PENGUIN

SAHIBS' INDIA

Pran Nevile was born in Lahore and took his postgraduate degree there. After a distinguished career in the Indian Foreign Service and the United Nations, he decided to become a freelance writer and specialized in the study of social and cultural history of India. His particular fascination with the visual and performing arts inspired him to spend many years researching in libraries and museums in the UK and USA.

Nevile has written extensively on Indian art and culture and also acted as a consultant for two BBC films on the Raj. He is the author of *Lahore: A Sentimental Journey, Love Stories from the Raj, Beyond the Veil: Indian Women in the Raj, Rare Glimpses of the Raj, Stories from the Raj: Sahibs, Memsahibs and Others, K.L. Saigal: Immortal Singer, Marvels of Indian Painting, Nautch Girls of the Raj* and *The Tribune—An Anthology 1881–2006.*

Sahibs' India

Vignettes from the Raj

PRAN NEVILE

PENGUIN BOOKS

PENGUIN BOOKS
Published by the Penguin Group
Penguin Books India Pvt. Ltd, 11 Community Centre, Panchsheel Park, New Delhi 110 017, India
Penguin Group (USA) Inc., 375 Hudson Street, New York, New York 10014, USA
Penguin Group (Canada), 90 Eglinton Avenue East, Suite 700, Toronto, Ontario, M4P 2Y3, Canada (a division of Pearson Penguin Canada Inc.)
Penguin Books Ltd, 80 Strand, London WC2R 0RL, England
Penguin Ireland, 25 St Stephen's Green, Dublin 2, Ireland (a division of Penguin Books Ltd)
Penguin Group (Australia), 250 Camberwell Road, Camberwell, Victoria 3124, Australia (a division of Pearson Australia Group Pty Ltd)
Penguin Group (NZ), 67 Apollo Drive, Rosedale, North Shore 0632, New Zealand (a division of Pearson New Zealand Ltd)
Penguin Group (South Africa) (Pty) Ltd, 24 Sturdee Avenue, Rosebank, Johannesburg 2196, South Africa

Penguin Books Ltd, Registered Offices: 80 Strand, London WC2R 0RL, England

First published by Penguin Books India 2010

Copyright © Pran Nevile 2010

10 9 8 7 6 5 4 3 2 1

ISBN 9780143066910

Typeset in Sabon by InoSoft Systems, Noida

Printed at Yash Printographics, Noida

To my grandchildren and their spouses—Gaurika
and Siddharth, Aditya and Pallavi, Anshuman
and Megha—for their love and support

Contents

Preface and Acknowledgements

Prefaces are believed not only to be the last part of a book to be written, but also the last which is read. I have no great stories to tell, nor can relate anything which others could not narrate as well. I am only a fact-finding author and can brag of nothing except my good intentions. My object has been to blend light reading for entertainment with historical information.

I come from a generation born and brought up during the heyday of the Raj. We studied *Simple Chapters of English Life*, a compulsory textbook for matriculation students. As regards the subject of history, our books had a chapter on the *'angrezi raj ki barkaten'*, or the blessings of English rule, and it was a standard question in the school examinations. We generally thought of sahibs as Englishmen, though they included the Irish, Scots and Welsh—the word Britisher was seldom used. It was through the spread of modern education that English thought, literature and political tradition were introduced to India.

As I began writing post-retirement, my foremost interest was to study Raj literature, comprising journals, memoirs, diaries and travelogues, in order to educate myself about the social and cultural life of the sahibs, who from traders had turned into empire builders. In these volumes I discovered revealing accounts of the changing patterns of the sahibs' social and cultural life in India and how the early East India Company civilians and soldiers had come under the spell of the Indian way of life. They took to hookah, arrack and Indian dress. They kept zenana, married native dusky beauties and became fond of the local sports of shikar, cockfights and animal fights. Also, they became keen patrons as well as spectators of nautch entertainment.

The English social life in the eighteenth and nineteenth centuries was obviously moulded by the current circumstances and political environment. Significant changes took place during the succeeding decades with the rising prestige and power of the Company Bahadur, as the East India Company came to be colloquially known by the Indian people. India was no longer depicted in the shadowy colours of Arabian Nights, with marble palaces of kings, their harems with beautiful damsels in gauzy veils dripping with pearls and diamonds, and the fabulous splendour of the courts. There were now some enlightened Englishmen, both officials and visitors, who looked beyond the poverty, the heat and dust, towards the spirit of the people, proud of their ancient civilization, culture and literature.

In recent decades, there has been a spate of books on the Raj. My wanderings in the field of Raj literature enabled me to write *Love Stories from the*

Raj, published in 1995. I also explored the vast visual record of paintings and sketches by both professional and amateur English artists who visited India during the eighteenth and nineteenth centuries. Housed mostly in the British Library and Museum and the Victoria and Albert Museum, London, this pictorial material brings a long-dead society back to life.

Most authors tend to believe that their work contains something new and different, not available in other books. It is my humble attempt to cover some of the untold stories of the Raj. The essence of history is not merely the study of events but also what people thought and said about them.

My research has taken me to several libraries and museums in Europe and the USA, but I have done most of my work in the British Library, London, and the US Library of Congress, Washington. I wish to express my gratitude to these great institutions for all the assistance I received from their courteous and helpful staff. I would like to express my grateful thanks to Dr P.J. Marshall, then professor of history at King's College, University of London, who in 1988 offered his valuable guidance and encouraged me to pursue my research in this field of study. I would also like to thank Professor Denis Judd, then professor of history at the North London University, who invited me to give lectures to his postgraduate students. I am equally indebted to Ian Talbot, then professor of South Asian studies at Coventry University and Robert L. Hardgrave, then professor of government and Asian studies at the University of Texas at Austin for their support and encouragement in my pursuits.

Finally, my grateful thanks go to Penguin Books for evincing interest in my work. Also a word of deep appreciation for Vaishali Mathur and Archana Shankar who diligently worked on the text and the selection of compatible illustrations and of course their editorial competence and genuine interest in the subject.

1

Household Retinue

It was the lure of wealth that brought Englishmen to India, the land of 'boiling sun and scorching wind'. With secure incomes, they took to lives of ease and luxury, in tune with the ostentatious lifestyle of the native aristocracy. They employed armies of servants for the comfort of their households and to establish their prestige and status in society. The new nabob had arrived on the Indian scene.

The picture of Englishmen in eighteenth-century India emerging from travel books and tales told by travellers was that they lived in grand bungalows, surrounded by the luxuries of oriental splendour. 'Troops of dusky white-clad servants stood near, with watchful regard awaiting the nod of their master, who buried in a pile of yielding cushions, gently breathed forth the fumes of perfumed tobacco from a jewelled hookah. At a sign from him cool sherbet and the "weepings of the Shiraz Vine" were brought by the ready attendants, and when in the evening he issued forth, gilded palanquins and a proud array of noble Arabian horses awaited his languid choice.'

The sahibs and memsahibs were expected to do nothing. Servants with specific duties waited on their masters. There were servants to pull off the sahibs' boots and maid servants to comb the memsahibs' hair. Domestic help would even pick up a handkerchief dropped on the floor. The Englishman's strongest link with the Indian world was through his servants who acquainted him with the customs and manners of the natives. Small wonder, there are numerous references to Indian servants in the literature of the period. Opinions about servants' character, honesty and loyalty differ but the common feeling was that good masters invariably managed to have good servants.

From the middle of the eighteenth century, John Company's officials took to living like aristocrats. The large retinue of servants had strict division of labour: each servant was employed for a specific task compatible with his caste functions. Besides, each servant had an assistant as per the established custom. Yet the large number in the employ of sahibs was no dearer than the few attending on wealthy families in England. Even the most junior officer had a team of servants as the pattern of social life followed by everyone required servants to uphold the position of their masters.

Philip Francis wrote in Warren Hastings's time that his cousin and he shared a house in Calcutta and had seventy servants between them. Fanny Parks, a famous traveller and author, found that she and her husband needed fifty-seven servants while William Hickey, not a wealthy man by Calcutta standards, had sixty-three. Some married couples maintained a staff of a hundred or more. Several servants had no work except to wait at the table, a dozen or more worked in the kitchen, and the same number worked as valets. There were grooms, coachmen, hairdressers, wig barbers, punkhawallas, maids for the ladies and ayahs for the children, washermen, gardeners, carpenters, tailors, palanquin-bearers, durwans, *chobdars*, peons and *hookahburdars*. Lady Nugent, wife of the commander-in-chief (1811), humorously observed that every servant appeared to have a servant. Each horse had not only a groom but a grass-cutter as well; every dog too had a boy to attend to him. A visitor enquired whether the cat had any servant, but he found that she was allowed to wait upon herself; and as she seemed the only person in the establishment capable of so doing, he respected her accordingly. In fact one visitor was surprised to find that there wasn't some menial to masticate his employer's food. A day in the life of an Englishman in Calcutta is thus described in a letter from a resident in Calcutta to his friend in London written on 23 December 1779 and included in *Macintosh's Travels* (1782):

> About the hour of seven in the morning, his durwan (doorkeeper) opens the gate and the veranda (gallery) is free to his circars, peons (footmen), hurcarrahs (messengers or spies), chubdars (a kind of constable), houccaburdars and consumahs (stewards and butlers), writers and solicitors. The head bearer and jemmadar enter the hall and his bedroom at eight o'clock. A lady quits his side and is conducted by a private staircase, either to her own apartment, or out of the yard. The moment the master throws his legs out of bed, the whole force is waiting to rush into his room, each making three salaams, by bending the body and head very low, and touching the forehead with the inside of the fingers and the floor with the back part. He condescends, perhaps, to nod or cast an eye towards the solicitors of his favour and protection. In about half an hour after undoing and taking off his long drawers, a clean shirt, breeches, stockings and slippers are put upon his body, thighs, legs and feet, without any

greater exertion on his own part than if he was a statue. The barber enters, shaves him, cuts his nails, and cleans his ears. The chilumchee and ewer are brought by a servant whose duty it is, who pours water upon his hands and face and presents a towel. The superior then walks in state to his breakfasting parlour in his waistcoat; is seated, the consumah makes and pours out his tea, and presents him with a plate of bread or toast. The hairdresser comes behind, and begins his operation, while the houccaburdar softly slips the upper end of the snake or tube of the hucca into his hand; while the hairdresser is doing his duty, the gentleman is eating, sipping and smoking by turns. By

A young civilian's toilet (by William Taylor, c.1840)

and by his banian presents himself with humble salaams and advances somewhat more forward than the other attendants. If any of the solicitors are of eminence, they are honoured with chairs. The ceremonies are continued perhaps till 10 o'clock; when, attended by his cavalcade, he is conducted to his palanquin, and preceded by eight to twelve chubdars, harcarrahs and peons, with the insignia of their professions and their livery distinguished by the colour of their turbans and cumurbands (a long muslin belt wrapt round the waist). They move off at a quick amble; the set of bearers, consisting of eight generally, relieve each other with alertness and without incommoding their master. If he has visits to make, his peons lead and direct the bearers; and if business renders his presence only necessary, he shows himself, and pursues his other engagements until two o'clock when he and his company sit down perfectly at ease in point of dress and address, to a good dinner, each attended by his own servant. And the moment the glasses are introduced regardless of the company of ladies, the houccaburdars enter, each with a houcca, and blowing the fire the whole time. As it is expected that they shall return to supper, at 4 o'clock they begin to withdraw without ceremony, and step into their palanquin; so that in few minutes, the man is left to go into his bedroom, when he is instantly undressed to his shirt, and his long drawers put on; and he lies down in his bed, where he sleeps till about 7 or 8 o'clock, then the former ceremony is repeated and clean linen of every kind as in the morning is administered; his houccaburdar presents the tube to his hand, he is placed at the tea table, and his hair-dresser performs his duty as before. After tea he puts on a handsome coat, and pays visits of ceremony to the ladies; returns a little before 10 o'clock; supper being served at 10. The company keep together till between 12 and 1 in the morning, preserving great sobriety and decency; and when they depart our hero is conducted to his bedroom, where he finds a female companion to

amuse him until the hour of 7 to 8 the next morning.
With no greater exertion than these do the Company's
servants amass the most splendid fortunes.

The following poem from *The Life and Adventures of
Shigram-Po* (Calcutta, 1821) presents a vivid picture of
a Sahib and his servants:

Here they rise very late and beginning to dress
Are surrounded by slaves for they can't do with less.
For the heat is so great that unfortunate elves
They've scarcely the pow'r to accountre themselves
So languid and weak, they are frequently known
To rise as fatigued as at night they laid down
Then the natives of India to cast do so cling
You scarcely get two to perform the same thing
One puts on stocking, one holds a serie
Another with chilumchee stands ready bye
A third has a mirror, he brings to your view
A fourth fellow is tying, the string of your shoe
Or perhaps undressing a bearer's undoing
Your shoes or cravat there is another champoeing
Your arms or your legs which'er he may lighten
Like famed Dean Mohmed champoes at Brighton

An English lady's life was equally leisure-oriented and
every comfort of hers was taken care of by her female
servants constantly in attendance. Memsahibs after their
stay in India had learnt the art of never moving from
their perch if they could avoid it.

They lie on a sofa, and if they drop their handkerchief,
they just lower their voices and say, 'Boy!' in a very gentle
tone, and then creeps in perhaps, some old wizen, skinny
brownie, looking like a superannuated thread-paper, who
twiddles after them for a little while, and then creeps out
again as softly as a black cat, and sits down cross-legged
in a verandah till 'Mistress please to call again'.

Emily Eden was bewildered by the number of servants attached to her. She wrote:

> An astonishingly agreeable khidmatgar and four others glide behind me whenever I move from one room to another; besides these, there are two bearers with a sedan at the bottom of the stairs, in case I am too idle to walk, but I have not trusted my precious person to their care yet. There is a sentry at my dressing room, who presents arms when I go to fetch my pocket handkerchief, or find my keys.

In the royal household of the viceroy, Lord Lytton, there were 300 indoor servants, of whom a third were cooks. They appeared in magnificent uniforms with glittering buttons and badges. Once there was an embarrassing slip-up when Lord Lytton embraced his head jemadar,

A young lady's toilet attended by ayahs (by William Taylor, c. 1840)

resplendent in gold and lace, mistaking him for a visiting raja. He complained that if he opened the door there were ten jemadars in red and gold livery 'crouching on the threshold', if he strolled along the corridors 'three unpronounceable beings in white and red nightgowns' pursued him; a discreet departure by the backdoor inevitably involved being 'stealthily followed by a tail of fifteen persons'.

The number of servants considered indispensable for a moderate establishment in other presidency towns of Bombay and Madras was nearly the same as in Calcutta.

A large number of servants accompanied their masters when they were on the move, even when they went to the battlefield. A captain in the Mysore campaign of 1780 'was joined by his butler, his cook, his valet, a groom with an assistant, a barber, a dhobi and others besides fifteen coolies to carry his luggage, his wines and liquor, live poultry and milch goats'.

The system of domestic service was very well organized with different departments of the establishment under the charge of professional experts. At the top of the list was the sarkar or dubash in Madras who helped the sahib settle down, found him a house and servants and, if needed, even procured a 'sleeping dictionary', a native mistress from whom the sahib would pick up the local language. The sarkar controlled the financial side of the household, which gave him power over the servants and also over his master as he arranged the loans for him. He did not usually draw any regular salary but took about 5 per cent commission on the total turnover of all payments. After him came the khansama who played the role of a butler and controlled the under-kitchen servants, usually selected and appointed by him. He was supposed to be the master of culinary art and skilled in lining up exotic food on a well-laid-out table. His wages varied from eight to as high as twenty-five rupees per month, depending on his experience and calibre. Further, as he made all daily purchases in the bazaar, he received a modest commission or dustooree (from dustoor, or custom). This was an established practice and he would resent any insinuation that this was not a proper thing to do. When submitting accounts he would make a deliberate miscalculation in his own favour, depending upon the carelessness, helplessness or gullibility of his employer.

Next in hierarchy came the khidmatgar whose chief function was to bring food to the table in an orderly manner and be in attendance. Among the well-to-do families, there was a khidmatgar for each member and sometimes even two, but the usual domestic complement was two or three. Bachelors of moderate means had a single khidmatgar who took care of the master's person, wardrobe and apartment. The khidmatgars dressed in liveries with white turbans and, surmounted by the crest of the family, accompanied their masters to all public and private parties and stood behind each chair. His wages varied from six to ten rupees per month and were, at times, somewhat higher in fashionable houses, where late dinner and supper parties demanded more work and attention. He was an aspirant to the position and emoluments of a khansama. Next to him was the bawurchee or cook who was either a Muslim, a Portuguese, a Mug or a Hindu of a low caste. The Mugs, from the borders of Burma, were considered heaven-born cooks. The wages of a cook depended not so much on the rank of the master but his love of good living for which some men were willing to pay twice the average wage of six to twelve rupees. The cook was assisted by a mushalchee, literally the 'torch-bearer', such being his real work when travelling with his master, but in the household he was a dishwasher who earned four rupees a month. Next on the rolls of the domestic corps, was the head bearer or sirdar assisted by house-bearers and under-bearers. The duties of bearers depended upon the rank, wealth and habits of the master. As a personal servant, he helped his master dress up and took charge of the stores and all his property. In short, he served married or single men, as a *valet de chambre*. He also supervised the cleaning of furniture, dusting of rooms, making of beds and trimming of lamps, by his under-bearers. The wages of a sirdar varied from six to ten rupees and his assistants were given four to six rupees.

Next came the durwan or gatekeeper, an imposing figure in impressive attire, who was responsible for what went into and out of the house. After parties, he used to search the visitors' servants. There were also a number of other servants. The garden was in the charge of the mali (gardener) and the domestic corps included the coachman for every carriage, syce (groom) for every horse, ghaskot (grass-cutter), bhisty (water-carrier), mehtar (sweeper), the punkhawala for pulling the punkha or fan, and the chowkidar (watchman). If the master possessed a boat, he would also employ a manjhi or steersman, a goleeah or bowman and a number of dandys or rowers. Those who maintained private palanquins had a separate set of bearers to carry them from place to place. There were also a number of occasional or part-time servants attached to houses. These included the dhobi (washerman), the darzi (tailor) and the hajaam (barber).

For the memsahib, a servant of particular importance was the ayah who acted as a lady's maid in addition to looking after babalog or children. Often one ayah was engaged for each child. Her attachment to the mistress was proverbial, and love for the children a byword of oriental loyalty. She also acted as an informer and conveyed all the neighbourhood gossip to her memsahib. For breastfeeding of infants, amahs or wet nurses were employed. Their wages were in the range of seven to ten rupees per month.

This muster roll of servants makes up a list of those considered indispensable. There were a few others in the service of the opulent or the old-fashioned. The most conspicuous was the hookahburdar who attended to the sahib's hookah, blew on the charcoal and renewed the rose water. He accompanied his master to parties even at the Government House in Calcutta where the hookahburdars would enter in solemn procession, each taking up his position close to his master, to whom he handed the ivory mouthpiece after unwinding the coil of piping from round the neck of a hookah. He earned five to eight rupees a month. As the nineteenth century progressed, the oriental practice of hookah smoking declined. The hookah was replaced by the cheroot or cigar. By the middle of the century the hookahburdar had almost faded away from the scene. Another special servant was abdar, responsible for cooling water, wines, beer and other table delicacies. He was the walking refrigerator of those days and went with his master to every dinner party for cooling the master's wine, using saltpetre in a container for the bottle. However, after the introduction of American ice in the 1830s, his specialized services were no longer required and he was transferred to attend at the table on a salary of six to eight rupees a month. Another functionary, known by various appellations such as chuprasee, hurkarah, piyada, or peon, carried messages to and fro; in the absence of telephones, all communications with friends and neighbours were conducted by chits. Then there was the chubdar or umbrella-carrier. Both the chuprasee and chubdar were dispensed with in early nineteenth century.

The last of these extra hands was the jemadar, retained by gentlemen of status who had no time or interest to attend to anything other than their official business. He was a kind of domestic overseer and general confidential assistant who acted on ceremonial occasions as a gentleman usher. His wages were as high as sixteen rupees a month.

Before the abolition of slavery in 1789, some of the servants were technically slaves and could be bought or sold in the market. In some cases they were even branded like horses by their owners. The slaves were chiefly Malays and Coffrees of African origin as observed in contemporary advertisements in the *Calcutta Gazette*. In 1781, the following advertisement appeared: 'To be sold a fine Coffree boy, that understands the business of a butler, & c. Price four hundred sicca rupees. Gentlemen may see him by applying to the printer.'

European servants were few indeed and far from successful in Bengal. At times, sailors deserted ships to take up more remunerative employment as butlers and stewards with wealthy merchants and officials. They were also engaged to supervise and train Indian servants in accord with the European lifestyle. A European coachman was considered useful for the proper upkeep of the carriage, imported at great cost from England or France. They were, however, found to be rather expensive as they needed a house and servants of their own. Besides, they were not dependable as they would quit without notice and set up their own small business for which there were ample opportunities. Another handicap was their ability to understand conversations at the dinner table which gave them opportunities for mischief making. European women were no better as servants because they often deserted on finding a husband.

Indian servants and ayahs were also taken by the sahibs to England on their return home. This practice began in the eighteenth century. The reasons were many: 'a reluctance to leave behind a favourite, faithful servant, a wish to recreate the nostalgic splendour of Indian life in England, to minister to the needs of the family and children, during the long and arduous sea voyage back—an ayah was considered to be an expert in this or merely as a status symbol or curiosity.' Many families going to India preferred to hire in England Indian servants who were keen to return home. The ayahs were in great demand and in the course of time, a well-organized network was set up in London with an ayah's home in London's East End. Some ayahs travelled between Britain and India many times; one of them was reported to have made fifty-four round trips.

By and large, Indian servants were reasonably well treated by their masters. It was a kind of feudal relationship that was accepted and well established. Some gentlemen complained bitterly about their laziness and dishonesty, while others dubbed them thieves. In affluent families, many masters either ignored or failed to detect petty thefts and this induced some servants to indulge in cheating for a little gain. In not-so-affluent households, such misdemeanour caused irritation and dismissal. The following verse about a servant who stole his master's liquor is taken from *Lays of Ind*, a nineteenth-century classic illustrative of English life in India:

The Faithful Abboo

Abboo was a trusty servant,
Trusted by his master much;
And the latter's prayers were fervent
That he might have many such.

For whenever master thought his
Liquor disappeared a bit,
Abboo regularly caught his
Brother menials prigging it.

Always nailed some erring brother,
Got him sent away, or fined;
Abboo would have nailed his mother—
Abboo'd such an honest mind.

And his master, Colonel Jervis,
Honoured Abboo, raised his pay;
Loved him for his faithful service,
Hunting all the thieves away.

One by one they came and vanished,
One by one they came to grief;
Maties, chockras, peons were banished;
Still there always was a thief.

Mahlee, dhobie, cook, horsekeeper,
Each were to the chokee sent,
Last of all the wretched sweeper—
Still the Colonel's liquor went.

'Devilish odd this!' said the Colonel
'What a land to soldier in!
Abboo, this is most infernal—
Who the blazes drinks my gin?'

'How I tell, sar, Plenty thieves, sar;
Other servants bobbery pack,
Drinking up what master leave, sar,
Moment Abboo turn his back.

'Abboo found out plenty rogue, sar,
Stealing, 'busing master's name;
Master taking same-like logue, sar—
What I doing?—plenty shame.'

One fine night a dreadful yelling
Roused the Colonel. By-and-bye,
Frightened servants ran in telling
'Abboo—belly paining—die!'

In the pantry, groaning, shouting,
On the floor poor Abboo rolled;
And a bottle, past all doubting,
Abboo's sad disaster told.

Many bottles, on the table,
Odorous of gin were found;
But one bottle, with the label
'Kerosine' lay on the ground.

In the hurry of the minute
And the dark, he'd drained it clean,
Thinking master's gin was in it,
Dreaming not of kerosine.

For space in sircar service
Abboo did his wits employ
Never more will Colonel Jervis
Trust another native boy.

There were cases of maltreatment of servants where
they were severely beaten. William Russell, a *Times*

correspondent who visited India in 1858, was shocked
to see two native servants, bleeding, covered with
bandages lying on their charpoys (beds) moaning. But
in many homes, there was a bond of mutual trust
and understanding between servants and masters. Rev.
Acland (1847), in his account, praises his servants for
their honesty, loyalty and devotion. Several writers have
praised Indian servants. They were described as 'patient,
forebearing and quiet in their demeanour'. A little
kindness towards them was enough to gain their respect,
attention and even attachment. There were instances when
they followed their masters on foot and came in after a
journey of six or seven hundred miles cheerfully. Their
reverential and submissive conduct invited the observation
that they 'seem to have been created for the sole purpose
and sole ambition of serving the Europeans'.

Murray's *Handbook of India* (1859) refuted the
allegation that Indian servants lacked loyalty and
integrity. 'Pay them well and treat them well, and in
general they will be found more faithful and attached
than English domestics.' During the Mutiny, many Indian
servants lost their lives trying to protect the English
families they worked for. It was recognized that good
masters always found good servants. 'Thou shalt do
nothing for thyself which thy servant can do for thee'
was an unwritten law which was responsible for the
sahib's envied state of ease and feudal dignity. This led
someone to declare, 'they were the finest servants in the
world'. Many a sahib and memsahib realized the truth
of this only when they returned home.

2

Sex and the Sahib

The burgeoning Raj was a masculine affair. Women were honoured in their absence and the founders of the empire suffered prolonged separation from wives and families. To rephrase a hoary catchphrase, it may be said that the 'empire was not acquired in a fit of absence of mind, so much as in a fit of absence of wives'. According to Ronald Hyam, a British historian, 'the enjoyment and exploitation of black flesh was as powerful an attraction as any desire to develop economic resources . . .' In the exotic realms of Hindustan, many merchants and adventurers found outlets for their surplus emotional and sexual energy, somewhat suppressed in more inhibited Britain, where sex was regarded as a curse stemming from the original sin, and penalties for extramarital affairs and sexual deviation were severe.

Deterred by the dangers of a long and tortuous voyage, few British women ventured to come to India. The original charters of the East India Company forbade women on its posts. The Portuguese, who had preceded the British, used to send annual batches of women for marriage to their officials in Goa. British settlers initially married widows and daughters of Portuguese Catholics, which did not find favour with the East India Company. So, towards the end of the seventeenth century, the Company copied the Portuguese practice and shipped batches of young women divided into 'gentlewomen' and 'others' for the marriage mart in India. They were provided with free board and lodging for one year. As the demand for wives was far in excess of supply, some of the women took to prostitution as a more lucrative and possibly pleasant vocation than marriage. For this 'scandalous' behaviour, they were warned to mind their morals; otherwise they were to be fed on bread and water and shipped back home.

The experiment of importing women was not a happy one and the Company abandoned it in the eighteenth century, leaving its servants to find women for themselves. The civilians and soldiers were in a way encouraged to take native wives and mistresses. The general moral tone of the settlers was far from laudable. Parson Benjamin Adams (c. 1710) laments the immoral lives and debauched manners of some of his countrymen. He bemoans the incestuous as well as adulterous marriage of Sir Nicholas Waite, president of the Company at Surat, with his niece, and that of William Warren, Company surgeon at Calcutta, with a widow when he was already married but had left his wife at home.

Until the end of the eighteenth century, the number of European women was so small that every spinster or widow would be snapped up at once, irrespective of her physical charms. Around 1790, there were only 250 European women in Calcutta but 4,000 men. It was, therefore, normal practice for sahibs to keep Indian bibis or set up zenanas, an Indian solution to their sexual isolation. The Indian bibi, an unofficial wife or a long-time consort, dominated the sexual life of sahibs until the third decade of the nineteenth century. A favourite after-dinner toast was 'a lass and a lakh a day', a goal natural to men who saw a lakh of rupees a proper object of ambition and a bibi as a fitting companion. There was nothing shameful or secret about these liaisons and even the Governor General, Sir John Shore (1793–98), and the governor of Bombay and members of his Council publicly kept native women.

For the English nabob, having made a fortune, a large zenana became a status symbol. Some of them came to the conclusion that a hundred wives were better than just one, the whole lot being more faithful than one. An elderly army major merrily described his zenana consisting of sixteen Indian girls of all sorts and sizes. He reckoned that the expenses of his mistresses were much less than those required for maintaining an English wife. David Ochterlony, the British resident in Delhi (1803) popularly known as 'Loony Akhtar', lived like a royal prince and used to take the air in the evening accompanied by his thirteen Indian bibis riding elephants. According to Victor Jacquemont, a French visitor, his host in Delhi, William Frazer, the British commissioner (1830s), maintained seven Indian wives who lived together some distance away from Delhi, and he had many children who were all Muslims or Hindus depending upon the faith of their mothers. One Meadows Taylor of Sholapur had a harem of native beauties and all the girls were in competition to win his favour but he was particularly enchanted with a fifteen-year-old Maratha girl.

Resorting to native mistresses was not only a piece of erotic expediency, but these 'sleeping dictionaries' were considered a delightful method of learning the language, customs and manners of the people. Some sahibs have left interesting accounts of their impressions about Indian women. Both Captain Mundy and Captain Skinner (1830s) were elated by the sight of 'upright', supple and slender well-rounded limbs of Hindu girls and their smooth skin of a bright chestnut colour. They keenly watched them bathing in the Ganges or drawing water at wells. The famous Sir Richard Burton who was in western India from 1842 to 1848 displays with obvious zest his knowledge of Sindhi women and his personal responses to their physical attraction and feminine charms. From these accounts, one may infer that the authors must have had some temporary or regular liaisons with native women.

The most unequivocal confession of having had a sexual relationship with an Indian woman is by William Hickey, a famous attorney in Calcutta (1790s). In his fascinating memoirs, he relates how after his initial hesitation, he finally succumbed to the charms of a dusky beauty procured by his servant. Later he took as his bibi the 'lovely Jemdanee, as gentle and affectionately attached a girl as ever man was blessed with' and has left a moving account of his life with her. Samuel Brown, a Company official, recorded in his journal (c. 1838), 'The native women were so amusingly playful, so anxious to please, that a person after being accustomed to their society shrinks from the idea of encountering the whims, or yielding to the furies of an Englishwoman.' Sir Garnet Wolseley, who was in India just after the Mutiny, confessed to his brother that he managed to console himself with a beautiful 'Eastern princess' who 'answered all the purposes of a wife without giving any of the bother'. So he had no wish to be caught in a European marriage to 'some bitch' unless she was an heiress.

Dr John Shortt, Company surgeon in Madras in the latter half of the nineteenth century, was charmed by the grace and beauty of Telugu girls. He wrote: 'I have seen several of these girls in my professional capacity, while they lived as mistresses with European officers, and have been greatly surprised at their ladylike manner, modesty and gentleness, such beautiful small hands and little taper fingers, the ankles neatly turned, as to meet the admiration of the greatest connoisseur . . . this is not to be wondered at that these girls were preferred to their own countrywomen.'

There was an army colonel who even agreed to be circumcised in order to get possession of a Muslim woman who imposed this condition before becoming his mistress.

Captain Williamson, who spent twenty years in the Company's service in India, in his famous guidebook *East India Vade Mecum* (1810) justified the practice of keeping Indian mistresses as being far more economical than maintaining European wives and as demanded by the exigency of the situation of expatriate bachelors. Williamson says nothing explicit about his personal experience but speaks eloquently about his familiarity with the ways of the zenana. He observes, 'Young men attach themselves to the women of the country and acquire a liking or taste for the society and customs which soon supersedes every other attraction.' In regard to the expenses of keeping a native mistress, Williamson adds, 'They will depend on the circumstances, and the disposition of the gentleman, generally speaking—a certain sum to be paid monthly: the pay of two or three female attendants, an allowance for betel; tobacco, shoes, clothes and gold and silver ornaments.' He estimated the whole cost at forty rupees a month 'which must certainly be considered no great price for a bosom friend, when compared with the sums laid out upon some British damsels'.

For the greater part of the eighteenth century, the Company's servants were merchants come to India in search of fortunes. Some sahibs also casually patronized other women of pleasure as referred to in the satirical poem 'Adventures of Qui Hi' (1816) (Koi hai—'is anyone there?', a European's call to his servants):

> Here serious characters resort
> And quit domestic broils for sport,
> And in some sooty fair one's arms
> Forget sweet matrimony's charms.

Towards the beginning of the nineteenth century, British women started arriving in India in increasing numbers. This led to incessant pressure for the abandonment of bibis. Englishwomen saw bibis as a threat to their position and succeeded in persuading the men to distance themselves from native connection. Over the years, they inculcated a feeling of racial superiority and by the middle of the nineteenth century, liaisons with native women were frowned upon and concubinage was morally outlawed. After the 1857 Mutiny, the practice virtually died out.

Englishwomen came in search of husbands with wealth and position. Many young girls therefore married men twice their age, who showered them with jewels, costly clothes and carriages to win their love. Many alliances were also concluded in utter haste, without knowledge of the family background of prospective bridegrooms. Devoid of attachments, many such ill-matched unions led to illicit affairs and scandals. Young civil and military officials, without the financial means to afford a European wife, were ever willing to offer their services and pay their homage to the fashionable married women, who looked for amours outside wedlock.

As the nineteenth century rolled on, the British established a chain of civil and military stations and their social life came to revolve within the community. They had their exclusive clubs for entertainment and enjoyment. As to their sex life, it is difficult to determine the truth in the accusation that they committed adultery without compunction. At home, the Victorian standard of morality was quite strict. There was a general impression that British society in India was immoral and women were the target of most of the criticism. Husbands and wives spent long periods of time apart from each other, giving opportunities for extramarital affairs.

Flirting with the other sex was normal in British social life in India. Though considered a harmless game, there were occasions when it led to adultery followed by gossip and scandals. One regiment, known for its enthusiastic adultery, was labelled the 'Fornicating Fifth'. For sexual escapades of a more exciting kind there were hill stations which offered plenty of opportunities for fun to lonely wives and civil and military men on leave. Frank Richards, who served as an ordinary soldier in India before the First World War, felt that it was almost impossible for the young and pretty wife of a soldier to remain faithful to her husband if she were sent to the hills on her own.

The open lifestyle in a close-knit community gave ample scope for rumours and gossip. It was proclaimed that the only way in India to keep adultery a secret was to commit it on the night mail train!

Prostitution did not lag behind in meeting the sexual needs of the sahibs. Lal bazaars (red-light districts) functioned in all presidency towns and cantonments. Measures were taken to register and supervise the prostitutes visited by Europeans in order to prevent the spread of venereal disease. White women, chiefly from eastern Europe, as well as Japanese girls procured to staff the brothels in Calcutta and Bombay, were also patronized by the better-off sahibs. There were also freelance operators. Among the white women resident in India, some of those divorced by their husbands and unable to return home, ashamed of the disgrace they had brought upon themselves, took to the flesh trade.

The brothels in the cantonments were usually supervised by an elderly madam who was paid her fees from the regimental funds. Indian men were not permitted to enter the brothels visited by the British soldiers. If caught, they were beaten up and thrown out. Sex was quite cheap; the standard rate in cantonments was one rupee for a sergeant, eight annas for a corporal, six for a lance corporal and four for a private. There was an instance when the commanding officer of a regiment asked the cantonment magistrate or kotwal to provide an adequate number of young and attractive women to be housed in the brothel area of the Regimental Bazaar. He complained that he had only six women for four hundred men, and calculated that he needed six more.

The missionaries protested and wanted prostitutes to be evicted from cantonment areas, but the official view was that prostitution fulfilled a socially necessary function and their removal might lead to offences such as criminal assault, rape, etc. The military authorities considered it dangerous to deny men sexual outlets. The Indian press fully supported the official stand and according to one weekly paper, 'not to provide women for European soldiers who are drunk and mad with lust would be like letting loose beasts of prey.' However, the English moralists' pressure continued and by the turn of the twentieth century army brothels were officially forbidden although commanding officers frequently made discreet but strictly unofficial arrangements for their men.

In Bombay, the missionaries started the 'Midnight Mission' (1890s) to patrol the European brothel area shouting slogans like 'Be sure, your sin will be found out.' This led to frequent brawls and missionaries were assaulted both by the prostitutes and their white clients. Eventually they were driven out by the police under a court order which stated that misguided missionaries could not be allowed to invade the streets at night and interfere with the rights and liberties of the public. The missionary zeal for imposing morality was completely ineffective and the sex trade in different forms continued to thrive. In any case the escapades of sahibs were of little consequence and did not in anyway impair the supremacy of the Raj.

3

Memsahibs and the Indian
Marriage Bazaar

Until the late eighteenth century very few British women ventured to India. It was a male-dominated society where ladies played only a subsidiary role. The age of the memsahib began with the introduction of the overland route and the steamship in the 1830s, was fortified with the opening of the Suez Canal in 1869 and lasted until the end of the Raj. The memsahibs inculcated a feeling of racial superiority and brought 'little England' to India. They enjoyed socializing with their own kind and were largely cut off from contact with real India.

Memsahibs then did not share the scruples of later generations and showed due respect for native lifestyle and customs. They had no objection to the hookah and occasionally smoked it while the dames were on exhibition. Around 1800, there were only two hundred and fifty European women in Bengal and its dependencies as against four thousand men. The cost of landing a European wife in Calcutta worked out to Rs 5,000—far beyond the means of ordinary Company officials. On the other hand, according to Captain Williamson's guidebook published in 1810, the expenses that had to be incurred on an Indian mistress, worked out to Rs 40 per month.

However, things did change and in that era of large families in England the only prospect for girls without dowry or physical beauty was spinsterhood. More and more English women started coming to the great Indian marriage bazaar. Moreover, as British settlers acquired wealth and power, the memsahibs began arriving on the scene in search of rich husbands. Men who had amassed fortunes in India (called nabobs) were much sought after by the parents and guardians of marriageable daughters. Even as early as in Robert Clive's time, girls just out from home were known as the 'newly arrived angels' and there was great competition to get them ashore at Madras or to escort them from their carriages to the church in Calcutta.

As the nineteenth century rolled on, English ships brought regular cargoes of venturesome beauties bent on matrimony, growing into a social phenomenon called the 'Fishing Fleet'. With this influx of women, Edinburgh came to be called the 'flesh market for the Indian marriage mart'. London sent out supplies too. It was an age of quick marriages. The arrival of a cargo of young damsels was one of the exciting events for the waiting bachelors in India. To keep them chaste for the marriage market, unmarried women travelled under the care of chaperones, usually married women who were making the voyage to join their husbands. The age, height, manners, features and fashionable dresses of the young women became topics of conversation. On such occasions, the captains of the ships and other well-known ladies of the settlement would organize parties and the candidates for wifehood sat up, as it was called, for three or four nights in succession while the eligible bachelors, young and old, tried their luck. Matches were arranged on the spot while the dames were on exhibition.

The church on Sundays was also a recognized marriage bazaar where the cargo of beauties appeared in splendour while the gallants waited on the steps of the church to greet them. They received proposals from all gentlemen, both known and not known. The greater part of the cargo was disposed of quickly. What was left of the Fishing Fleet sailed to the mofussil areas to scoop up husbands from the unmarried officials, soldiers, planters and businessmen. With such a multitude of wife-seekers, the woman had to be very unattractive or overambitious not to find a catch and join the group of 'Returned Empties', a term used for those returning to England without husbands.

The attention and court paid to these Englishwomen was astounding, as recorded by Sophia Goldbourne:

> My smile was meaning and my articulation melody; in a word, mirrors are almost useless in Calcutta and self-adoration for your looks is reflected in the pleasures of every beholder and your claims to first-rate distinction confirmed by all who approach you.

Another lady in Calcutta writing to her friend spoke about the hardships of her sea voyage and then narrated:

> And yet, dear girl! this place has charms,
> such as my sprightly bosom warms!
> No place where at a bolder rate
> We females bear our sovereign state.
> Beauty ne'er points its arms in vain,
> Each glance subdues some melting swain.

Poet Thomas Hood was so struck by this traffic that he satirizes the ambitious husband-hunters in a malicious poem which begins:

> By Pa and Ma I'm daily told
> To marry now's my time.
> For though I'm very far from old,
> I'm rather in my prime.
> They say while we have any sun
> We ought to make our hay—
> And India has so hot a one
> I'm going to Bombay . . .

It ends with:

> My heart is full, my trunks as well,
> My mind and caps made up,
> My corsets shaped by Mrs Bell
> Are promised ere I sup;
> With boots and shoes, Riverta's best
> And dresses by Duce,
> And a Special Licence in my chest—
> I'm going to Bombay.

Victor Jacquemont, a French botanist visiting India at the time was not much impressed by the English ladies he met in Calcutta and in other places. He wrote (1830): 'Portionless girls who have not succeeded in getting married in England arrive here in cargoes for sale on honourable terms, I mean to young civil and military officers.'

Another Frenchman, Captain Edouard Warren, who served as an army officer in the East India Company, considered the parents' calculations of cost, risks and rewards rather sordid. He describes how the girls were advised by their aunts not to dance with anyone below the rank of a first-class civilian or military officer who could provide three essential things for happiness of conjugal life in India: a massive silver teapot, a palanquin and a set of bearers to use by day, and a carriage in which to drive in the evening. Following such advice, the girl would foolishly refuse some really eligible wooers of whom she would not have dreamt in England and succumb to the advances of some old nabob with spindle legs in whose mummy there was not a spark of heat and whose soul for the past twenty years had been concentrated on rupees.

A swarm of admires hover around Miss C's carriage at the bandstand (by G.F. Atkinson, c. 1856)

In such a situation many girls became accomplished flirts. As long as the girl made a suitable catch in the end, flirting was accepted as a pleasant activity except when the girl overdid it. The young civilian was considered a prime catch—three hundred pounds a year dead or alive; the East India Company provided an allowance of three hundred pounds a year on marriage to a civilian and on his death a pension for the same amount was given to the widow.

Considering the prevailing circumstances, it is not surprising that many girls adopted a somewhat mercenary attitude to the whole matrimonial procedure, which is reflected in their letters and journals. The following letter taken from *Macintosh's Travels* was addressed by a lady to her cousin in 1779 who had desired to be told the result of her cousin's adventures and to give advice on whether it would be fit for her to try the same experiment.

My dearest Maria,

With respect to your request that I should tell you plainly what I think of these matrimonial schemes (for such they are, let people disguise them as they will), I never can impress upon you too strongly the folly and impropriety of your making such an attempt. Certainly, the very project itself is one of the utmost delicacy; for what is but running counter to all the dictates of that diffidence and native modesty for which English women have been so long held up as the perfect models?

True it is that I am married; I have obtained that for which I came out to India—a husband; but I have lost what I left behind in my native country—happiness. Yet my husband is rich, as rich, or richer, than I could desire; but his health is ruined, as well as his temper, and he has taken me rather as a convenience than as a companion; and he plays the tyrant over me with as much as if I were one of the slaves that carry his palanquin . . . What a state of things that, where the happiness of a wife depend upon the death of that man who should be the chief not the only source of her felicity. However such is the fact in India; wives are out with gratitude for the next mortality that may carry off their husbands, in order that they may return to England to live upon their jointures;

they live a married life, an absolute misery, that they may enjoy a widowhood of affluence and independence. This is no exaggeration I assure you.

You know that, independent of others, there were thirty females on board the H, who sailed upon the same speculation; we were of all ages, complexions and sizes, with little or nothing in common, but that we were single, and wished to get married. Some were absolutely old maids of the shrivelled and dry description, most of them above the age of fifty; while others were mere girls just freed from the tyranny of the dancing, music, and drawing masters at boarding schools, ignorant of almost everything that was useful, and educated merely to cover the surface of their mental deformity. I promise you, to me it was no slight penance to be exposed during the whole voyage to the half-sneering, satirical looks of the mates and guinea pigs, and it would have been intolerable, but for the good conduct and politeness of Captain S. He was a man of most gentlemanly deportment, but the involuntary compassion I fancied I sometimes discovered in him, was extremely irksome. However, we will suppose our voyage ended, for nothing at all material happened, and that we are now safely landed at Calcutta.

This place has many houses of entertainment of all descriptions, and the gaiety that prevails after the arrival of a fleet from England is astonishing. The town is filled with military and civil officers of all classes; and the first thing done after we have recovered our looks, is for the captains to give an entertainment, to which they issue general invitations; and everybody with the look and attendance of a gentleman, is at liberty to make his appearance. The speculative ladies, who have come out in the different ships, dress themselves with all the splendour they can assume, exhausting upon finery all the little stock of money they have brought out with them from Europe. This is in truth their last, or nearly their last stake, and they are determined to look and dance as divinely as possible.

Rival candidates for matrimony, Calcutta (by James Moffat, c. 1800)

Such are the majority of the ladies; while the gentlemen are principally composed of those who have for some time resided in the country, and having realised fortunes, are determined to obtain wives with as little delay as possible. They are, as I have said, of all ranks, but generally of pale and squalid complexions, and suffering under the grievous infliction of liver complaints. A pretty prospect this for matrimonial happiness! Not a few are old and infirm, leaning upon sticks and crutches, and even supported about the apartment by their gorgeously dressed servants, for a display of all kinds of splendour on their part is no less of coyness or reluctance. In fact, this is the mode in which matches are generally made and if now and then one happy couple comes together, thousands are married with no hope of comfort and with a prospect merely of splendid misery. Generally speaking, in India, the officers make the best husbands, for they are frequently young and uninjured by the climate, and are the best disposed to attend to the wishes of their wives.

This is called the Captain's Ball, and most frequently the greater part of the expectant ladies are disposed of there; it is really curious, but most melancholy, to see them ranged round the room, waiting with the utmost anxiety for offers, envy upon all who are more fortunate than themselves.

If however, as is sometimes the case, a considerable number remain on hand, after the lapse of about three months, they unite in giving an entertainment at their own expense, to which all gentlemen are at liberty to go; and if they fail in this dernier resort, this forlorn hope, they must give up the attempt, and return to England.

Once a girl had been chosen it was time for the marriage. But the Governor General's licence to be married was necessary to constitute it a legal one. On the occasion of a marriage the officiating minister was accustomed to receiving as his fee between sixteen and twenty gold mohurs, and five gold mohurs for a baptism. No wonder that the chaplains were able to make such splendid fortunes in a short time.

Here is an extract from the *Lays of Ind* by Aliph Cheem, a collection of comic verse, which ran into several editions in the nineteenth century:

I do believe in dress and ease,
And fashionable dash.
I do believe in bright rupees,
And truly worship cash.

But I do believe that marrying,
An acting man is fudge;

And so do not fancy anything
Below a pucca judge.

I do believe that if I'm smart,
And do not lose my head
And cut that thing that's called the heart,
I may a fortune wed.

The Indian marriage market excited the imagination and ambition of generations of British girls. It was not unusual for a young girl to marry someone twice or even thrice her age. 'India is a paradise of middle-aged gentlemen,' wrote a lady from Madras in 1837. This was because young men in India 'thought nothing of being posted in remote areas to make or mar their fortunes' but at forty when they are 'high in the service, rather yellow, and somewhat grey, they begin to be taken notice of, and called "young men"'.

Marriage notices such as the following were inserted in the Calcutta papers: 'The marriage is announced of H. Meyer Esq. aged sixty-four to Miss Casina Coupers, a very accomplished young lady of sixteen after a courtship of five years.' Another read:

A young man of genteel connections and a pleasing appearance, being desirous of providing himself with an amiable partner and agreeable companion for life, takes this opportunity to solicit the fair hand of a young and beautiful lady: personal accomplishments are absolutely necessary, though fortune will be no object, as he is on the point of taking a long and solitary journey to a distant and remote part of the country, and is anxiously solicitous to obtain a partner of his pleasures and soother of his woes. A line addressed to Mr Atall, No. 100, Writers' Buildings, will meet with every possible attention and the greatest secrecy will not only be observed, but Mr Atall will have the pleasure of giving due encouragement to their favour. Calcutta, The 21st November 1808.

Girls betrothed in England also came to India after years of waiting for their fiancés, but this did not always lead to happy reunions. Sometimes the man 'no longer found the girl attractive' and dropped her, or if he had got married in the meantime, would convey his apologies and offer her all assistance in getting another husband. There were also occasions when the girl, after meeting someone on the voyage would have a change of heart and announce on arrival to the waiting aspirant that the engagement was off.

One also comes across some other amusing instances of matrimony. There was a colonel in Madras who got married in January and was presented with his firstborn in March! Another officer was cashiered for seducing an unmarried girl and then arranging her marriage with a brother officer. The most extraordinary case, however, was that of Sir Paul Joddrel, physician to the nawab of Arcot (1790s). 'He lived in Madras with his wife, a young niece by the name of Miss Cummings, and a child. After he had fixed the wedding of Miss Cummings with one Captain Charlise, it came to be known that the young one was Sir Paul's mistress, a fact with which Lady Joddrel was well acquainted, and that the child was Sir Paul's by Miss C.'

The demand for wives was so great that ladies who lost their husbands had no difficulty in replacing them. A widow got frequent proposals on the steps of the church after the burial of her husband. These speedy marriages were far from uncommon and there were even cases where a wife would engage herself to a suitor during her husband's illness.

One of the most famous much married women was Begum Johnson who got married at the age of twelve and took her fifth husband when she was nineteen. She died in 1812 at the age of 87 and was given a state funeral.

At times young wives with old husbands got involved in scandalous affairs with younger men and even eloped with them. Here is another verse from the *Lays of Ind*:

Colonel White was over forty;
Jane, his bride was seventeen;
She was also very naughty
For she loved a Captain Green!

O Elders! Your hell has begun
If at sixty you marry with youth,
And can't be persuaded that fun
May be coupled with virtue and truth!

Another poem tells of one Arabella Green who, acting on the advice of her parents, was seeking matrimony with the high and mighty and did not pay any attention to the proposals of young civilians and soldiers:

She waited; but collectors did
Not come in spooney shoals
And Session's judges must have slid
On purpose to the Poles.

No signs of brigadiers and not
A staff corps Colonel!—why,
It really looked as if the lot
Were growing scarce, or shy.

. . .

She did what braver folks must do—
She bowed to circumstance;
But husbands still kept out of view,
By some unkind mischance.

In sorrow now and soon in shame
Poor Arabella watched
The ruin of her little game
Oh how completely botched.

In the meantime her father is transferred back home and she has to pack up and return with him, joining the ranks of spinsters as described in the following verse:

O spins, be warned ere yet too late—
To coin don't wholly lean,
Unless you wish to meet the fate
Of Arabella Green.

4

Sketches of Life by Englishwomen Artists

The period from the late eighteenth to the mid-nineteenth centuries witnessed a remarkable flowering of British interest in India—in the people, history, literature, antiquities, customs and manners. This encouraged British professional artists to come to India in search of expected patronage and wealth. While most of them confined themselves to landscape painting and portraits of the ruling elite or history pictures of imperial interest, the women artists applied their talents to other domains and have bequeathed to us a valuable collection of drawings, water colours and sketches which provided interesting visual records of English life during the Raj and their perception of the Indian scene.

The women artists, though non-professional, were very talented: their works frequently reached high standards and were in no way inferior to those of professionals. They had received solid training in drawing and watercolour painting. In England those days, drawing formed an essential part of a liberal education for the upper and middle classes. A private drawing master was as common as a music teacher who gave lessons either in school or at home. Even professional artists in Calcutta gave drawing lessons to both men and women. The women artists of the Raj were also notable writers and their journals and letters are a valuable source of information about the social life of the white community during the period. The most famous among them were Fanny Parks, Emily Eden, S.C. Belnos and Marianne Postans.

Fanny Parks was an enthusiastic artist who travelled extensively during her twenty-four years of stay (1822–45) in India. She has left for posterity a two-volume journal called *Wanderings of a Pilgrim in Search of the Picturesque* (1850) which is profusely illustrated with her sketches and drawings. A few of her sketches and engravings are mediocre but many are colourful and alive and display her proficiency in the art. She even learnt Hindustani and has also signed her sketches in Persian script.

Fanny Parks had access to the zenana and met Indian ladies of rank who impressed her with their elegance and charm. The graceful demeanour of an ordinary Bengali woman interested her greatly and she made a lovely sketch which bears testimony to her artistic talent. She was greatly amused by the story of a jealous wife telling her husband, 'I wish I were married to a grass cutter' because he being so poor could afford only one wife. She sketched her own grass cutter from real life. The romanticized or idealized images of people and Indian scenes were vividly captured by her.

S.C. Belnos started her carrier as an amateur artist and won remarkable success as a lithographer. Not much is known about her personal life except that she was married to a French miniature artist J.J. Belnos. There is evidence of her close association with Bengal. Some art historians assume that she was of mixed parentage and was born or brought up in Bengal. In 1832 she published her first album of 'Twenty-four Plates Illustrative of Hindoo and European Manners in Bengal'. Regarded as a document of the social history of India, the album portrays facets of the daily life and pursuits of Indians and Europeans, people and places whom she observed closely. She was meticulous in studying every detail of the subject matter

Celebrating Holi (by S.C. Belnos, c. 1840)

and her pictures are therefore self-explanatory. The album includes two important testimonials; one from Graves C. Houghton, the then secretary of the Royal Asiatic Society, London, who praised her paintings for 'their truth and elegance and for making art subservient to nature'. The second testimonial from Raja Rammohan Roy applauds her work as 'so expressive and true to nature that the descriptions, however excellent, are scarcely necessary'.

A picture which has established the artist's talent to lasting fame is entitled 'A Nautch'. It depicts a nautch entertainment for the Europeans by a native aristocrat. This painting is resplendent with warm colours and highlights the dazzling costume and jewellery of the dancing girl as well as the posture of her graceful movement which Belnos has executed with delicate proficiency.

Her second album, 'Sandhya or the Daily Prayers of the Brahmans', published in 1851, depicts devout Hindus as their prayers are recited and various rites performed. It is a mature and serious subject for which Belnos undertook long and painstaking research.

Emily Eden, the sister of Lord Auckland, the Governor General (1836–32), was a notable writer and artist. She has left for posterity the remarkable three-volume album of nearly 200 studies entitled 'Watercolour Sketches of Princes and Peoples of India'. Most of the drawings in the album, however, concern the lives of the common people rather than those of the princes. During her travels from Calcutta to Lahore in her brother's suite, she continually sketched the interesting figures she encountered and wrote long letters to her sister which were published in London in 1866 under the title 'Up the Country'. Eden had taken lessons in England from the best drawing masters of the day. Judging from her work we find that she was an accomplished amateur artist and her talent for painting flowered under the Indian sun. She would sometimes, go out on an elephant in search of a sketch. Her special status enabled her to paint portraits of important people. She was greatly impressed by the court of Ranjit Singh and his bejewelled nobility and their portrayal by her is of great historical interest. Even horses, camels and elephants with colourful trappings formed attractive subjects for her watercolours and were included in her famous album published in 1884.

Emily Eden never got over a feeling of exile, but she was remarkably active and found solace in drawing. Her artistic and imaginative mind was inspired by the settings she viewed around her and some subjects which she described in her letters formed the material of her sketches. She also delighted in portraying her servants. She would say that 'every servant in the government house is a picture by himself'.

Marianne Postans, wife of a Company officer, spent several years in western India. A keen observer of the Indian scene and a prolific writer, she was also an amateur artist. During her residence at Bhuj in Kutch, she made drawings of places and people there which was then an almost unknown area. Some of these drawings were included as illustrations in her book, *Cutch, or Random sketches*, published in 1839. It provides an interesting visual record of people who inspired her artistic pursuit. Her work is not of any high order but as the scenes and peoples of Kutch were depicted for the first time, these aroused ample interest. Her portrayal of the Rao of Kutch, the native ruler, and his soldiers is quite attractive and colourful.

Not burdened by a sense of imperial mission, women artists, very much part of the Raj, had an open mind

A mercenary soldier, Cutch (by Marianne Postans, c. 1838)

and took genuine interest in depicting the country and its people. As their sketches and drawings were mostly meant for themselves and not for any competitive market, they were executed quite freely and are thus more intimate observations of the Indian scene.

5

Fanny Parks: An Inveterate Traveller

Enamoured of India with its picturesque landscape and natural beauty, diverse people in exotic costumes, festivals, rituals and rites, music and dance and even its cuisine, Fanny Parks is one of the most appealing chroniclers of Indian life and lifestyle in the first half of the nineteenth century.

Fond of wandering and adventure and unmindful of creature comforts, Fanny travelled extensively during her twenty-four-year stay in the country (1822–46) and recorded her experiences in a monumental two-volume journal entitled, *Wanderings of a Pilgrim in Search of the Picturesque*. A keen observer with an open mind, she felt at home with native people of different classes and evinced genuine interest in learning their way of life, beliefs, and customs.

She learnt Persian and Hindi and used Hindi words, idioms and phrases extensively in her texts in order to give an oriental flavour to her expressions. Illustrated with sketches and paintings drawn by her, the journal is replete with lively eyewitness accounts of her encounters in India. Full of information on practically every aspect of the Indian social and cultural scene, her journal is a favourite document with Raj historians who recognize it as a classic, comparable with the works of famous India experts like Coryat, Roe, Bernier, Tavernier, and Manucci.

Fanny was a great admirer of the picturesque sights of India. She enjoyed participating in native festivities at river ghats and temples. She pursued visual beauty with greed, enjoying both 'the grandeur of storms' and the hurly burly scenes in towns and villages.

Born in England in 1794, this daughter of Captain William Archer married Charles Parks, an East India Company civilian and came with him to Calcutta in 1822. She was

> . . . a woman of boundless energy, both physical and mental, more than usually observant and inquiring, her interest not confined to the home or social life of the English stations. She was full of activity, taking a tremendous lot of exercise on horseback, exploring out of the way places and going on expeditions . . . She enjoyed danger, adventure, and solitude, and had no hesitation in setting off alone on long river journeys, for pleasure not necessity, in an unsuitable boat against the stream at the height of the rains or going in a rickety cart into the jungle to look for traces of a tiger.

She was equally impressed by the grandeur of the city of palaces and the luxurious lifestyle of the English civilians and soldiers. She wanted to discover mysterious India; while travelling in the north from Allahabad where her husband was stationed, she was captivated by the holy cities of Benares and Mathura and became an eager student of Hindu mythology and iconography. She gives graphic descriptions of the celebration of Hindu festivals and ceremonies.

Diwali celebrated on the ghats of Kanpur is made to come alive in her fascinating account (1830):

> On reaching the ghat,' she says, 'I was quite delighted with the beauty of a scene resembling fairyland . . . On every temple, on every ghat, and on the steps down to the river's side, thousands of small lamps were placed from the foundation to the highest pinnacle, tracing the architecture in the lines of light. The evening was very dark, and the whole scene was reflected in the Ganges.

She describes how crowds of Hindu worshippers prostrated themselves before the idols of Lord Shiva and Ganesha and then poured Ganges water, rice, oil, and flowers over the images of the gods. She also noted some women sending off little paper boats, each containing a lamp, which floating down the river, added to the beauty of the scene. The river was covered with fleets of these little lamps hurried by the rapid stream. She was so thrilled by the sight that she recorded, 'I was greatly pleased: so Eastern, so fairy-like a scene I had not witnessed since my arrival in India; nor could I have imagined that the dreary-looking station of Cawnpore contained so much of beauty.'

Fascinated by the legends of Krishna and his gopis, she made a study of the popular folklore on the worship of Krishna and Radha and collected an impressive stock of Hindu idols and artefacts which she claimed were far superior to what was held by the British Museum.

Fanny presents herself as a pilgrim to the East and in the Introduction to her journal she invokes the Hindu god Ganesha as the source of knowledge and learning and seeks his blessing in her venture. She writes:

O Ganesha thou art a mighty lord! Thy single tusk is beautiful and demands the tribute of praise from the Haji of the East. Thou art the chief of the human race; the destroyer of unclear spirits. The remover of fevers, whether daily or tertian! The pilgrim sounds they praise; let her work be accomplished.

Ganesha (by Fanny Parks, c. 1840)

She opens her journal with the well-known Indian proverb, 'Let the result be what it may, I have launched my boat.' Fanny also acknowledges that she became an ardent observer of Hindu customs and rites and sometimes her friends would tease her by saying, 'We expect someday to see you at puja by the river.'

Fanny was also enthusiastic about the charpai: 'It is the most luxurious couch imaginable, and a person accustomed to the charpai of India will spend many a restless night ere he can sleep with comfort on an English bed.' She also became fond of Indian cooking and preferred Indian food to European dishes. She even took a fancy for Indian-made dresses and admired Indian clothes, preferring the flowing lines of drapery to the vile round hats and stiff attire of the European gentlemen, and the equally ugly bonnets and stiff and graceless dresses of the English ladies.

Indeed, in the matter of dress Fanny became a complete Indophile. She writes:

> In Europe, how rarely—how very rarely does a woman walk gracefully! Bound up in stays, the body is as stiff as a lobster in its shell; that snake-like, undulating movement—the poetry of motion—is lost, destroyed by the stiffness of the waist and hip, which impedes the free movement of the limbs. A lady in European attire gives me the idea of a German manikin; an Asiatic, in her flowing drapery, recalls the statues of antiquity. English dresses are very unbecoming, both to Europeans and Asiatics. A Musulmani lady is a horror in an English dress; but an English woman is greatly improved by wearing a native one, the attire itself is so elegant, so feminine, and so graceful.

On a visit to England after seventeen years in India, she could not restrain her indignation at the female fashion of the times: She adds, 'What can be more ugly than the dress of the English? I have not seen a graceful girl in the Kingdom: girls who would otherwise be graceful are so pinched and lashed up in corsets, they have all and every one the same stiff dollish appearance; and that dollish form and gait is what is considered beautiful!'

Little wonder then that Fanny felt so at home with Indian society that she gives a delightful account of a 'dazzling party with nautch girls and musicians she attended at the house of a rich Bengallee baboo [sic]'. She also had the opportunity of witnessing the performance of Nickee, then the most celebrated nautch girl of Calcutta whom she describes as the 'Catalani of the East'. Her fancy for everything Indian led her to learn how to play the sitar. She describes how once some laughing slave girls at an Indian aristocrat's house danced merrily to a tune played by her on the sitar.

Like other Europeans, Fanny was also intrigued by the mysteries of the zenana where ladies of rank were secluded. She was easily the first memsahib to have an access to the zenana where she interacted with the ladies. They seem to have liked her for her warm and sympathetic curiosity and talked to her freely and informally.

Fanny studied the lifestyle and customs of these Indian ladies and even learnt the rules of Indian etiquette. Her intimacy with Colonel Gardener and the women of his family hailing from the Mughal nobility made her acquainted with the inner life of the zenana with all its intrigue, scandal and gossip. Enchanted by the graceful costumes of the ladies, she was particularly struck by the dupatta or the veil and writes: 'The *dopatta* is so transparent, it hides not; it merely veils the form adding beauty to the beautiful by its soft cloud-like folds. The jewellery sparkles beneath it and the outline of its drapery is continually changing according to the movements of coquetry of the wearer.'

Fanny's account of the interaction with the ladies of the Gardener household is both revealing and humorous. She also attended a grand family wedding and gives a detailed description of the elaborate wedding ceremonies and the mighty spectacle of the wedding procession with nautch girls dancing on moving platforms carried by men. She was amazed to find how fortunes were squandered by parents on the weddings of their daughters. Highly unconventional, Fanny had strong feelings about the position of women in society and the denial of education to them.

She also made friends with Baiza Bai, the deposed Maratha queen of Gwalior who impressed her far more than the exotic beauties of the zenana. She wrote, 'Her continence is very mild and open; there is freedom and independence in her air that I greatly admire.' Fanny supported Baiza Bai's political ambitions and they exchanged views about the universal oppression of women echoing the words of modern feminists. She visited Baiza Bai several times and 'liked her better than any native lady I ever met with'. She was impressed by the riding skills of Maratha women and found their method of sitting astride far more sensible than sitting on the side saddle. In her enthusiasm, and carried away by her emotions she even wrote, 'Were I an Asiatic, I would be a Maharatta.'

She gives a fascinating account of Janmasthmi (Lord Krishna's birthday festival) that she witnessed with Baiza Bai and her young princess who was amusing herself on the swing as a necessary part of the ceremony, 'after which some sixty or eighty Maharatta women came forward, and performed several dances sacred to the season, singing as they moved on the turf, in a circular dance called the rasa, in imitation of the *gopis;* and the *Songs of Govinda,* as addressed by Kaniya to Radha and her companions, were rehearsed at this festival, with a scenic representation of Kaniya and the *gopis.* The listener could not depart after once hearing the sound of the flute, and the tinkling of the *gopis'* feet; nor could the birds stir a wing; while the pupils of the *gopis'* eyes all turned towards Creeshna.'

Later, Fanny had the opportunity of calling on one of the Mughal princesses at the royal palace in Delhi. She was moved by the pitiable and impoverished state of these descendants of emperors. So much so, that out of compassion she refused to visit the chambers of Bahadur Shah. She found Delhi, once a magnificent city, just a heap of ruins dotted with the remains of extensive gardens, mosques and pavilions. This desolate sight incited Fanny to quote a couplet of Sadi, the famous Persian poet:

The spider has woven his web in the
royal palace of the Caesers,
The Owl standeth sentinel on the watch towers of
Afrasiab.

The irrepressible Fanny was shocked when she saw some European ladies and gentlemen with the band playing on the marble terrace of the Taj Mahal dancing in front of the tomb. She had admiration not only for the unearthly beauty of this wonderful monument but held it as a sacred edifice. She writes:

I cannot enter the Taj without feelings of deep
devotion: the sacredness of the place, the
remembrance of the fallen grandeur of the family of
the Emperor, and that of Asaf Jah, the father of
Arzumund Banoo. The solemn echoes, the dim light,
the beautiful architecture, the exquisite finish and
delicacy of the whole, the deep devotion with which
the native prostrate themselves when they make their
offering of money and flowers at the tomb, all produce
deep and sacred feelings; and I could no more jest
or indulge in levity beneath the dome of the Taj, than
I could in my prayers.

An extraordinarily high-spirited memsahib, Fanny Parks
shunned drawing-room gossip, needlework or playing
the piano and preferred less ladylike and adventurous
pursuits such as shikar, riding, stone-cutting, bird-stuffing
and, above all, exploring. She made several trips up and
down the Ganges and travelled to remote parts of the
country up to the Himalayas. In 1838 she wrote:

How much there is to delight the eye in this bright,
this beautiful world, roaming about with a good tent
and a good Arab, one might be happy forever in India.
I have a pencil instead of a gun and believe it affords
me satisfaction equal if not greater than the sportsman
derives from his Manton.

Besides giving an absorbing account of contemporary
British official and social life, Fanny's journal also
contains over forty full-page illustrations from her own
drawings and watercolours which display her proficiency
in the art. The romanticized or idealized images of
people and the views of Indian scenes have been vividly
captured by her with utmost fidelity and astonishing
detail. It is interesting to note that she inscribed her

signature on the sketches in the Persian script. In one case she points out that her picture of 'Kaniyajee and the Gopees is based on an original Hindoo painting'. It is indeed a superb replica of the original.

Once, she was greatly amused by the story of a native wife telling her husband in rage or jealousy, 'I wish I were married to a grass cutter' because he being so poor could afford only one wife. She sketched her own grass cutter from real life. Then, the graceful demeanour of an ordinary Bengali woman interested her greatly, so much so that she describes in detail her 'style of attire—the sari of muslin passed several times around the figure, a remarkably graceful dress'. She made a lively sketch of her with all the cosmetics and ornaments adorning her body. This is rated as one of her best sketches, testifying to her talent as an artist.

First published in 1850, Fanny's journal was reprinted in 1975 with an introduction and intensive notes by Esther Chawner who writes: 'In Fanny Parks we have the best of companions to introduce us to all the strangeness and novelty she found in India.' It is like a guided tour of the country, with its scenic splendour and panorama of life. She appears to have developed a double loyalty, to India and to England. Her writing is both witty and warm and is enriched with an exotic air and colourful detail. It is full of people, both European and Indian who come alive with her eyewitness accounts. She presents some rare and revealing glimpses of the days gone by. What she writes is always entertaining and much of it still remains interesting today.

6

The Amorous Adventures of
Lola Montez

Lola Montez belongs to that galaxy of renowned coquettes of history, the queens of elegance like Madame de Pompadour, Madame du Barry, Marie Antoinette, and Pauline Bonaparte who shared the glamour and glitter of royalty and enjoyed the power and prestige of the ruling elite. Besides their stunning beauty, grace and charm, these women were also endowed with a fiery intelligence and wit as well as some magical quality which cast a spell on men from all walks of life.

Their mesmerizing appeal was attributed as much to their brains as to their bodies. They had mastered the art of captivating men and never doubted their ability to drive away their rivals, if any, in this exciting game of love and passion. The daring amorous adventures of Mrs Thomas James, a very young memsahib of great beauty who created a sensation in Simla in 1839, makes for fascinating reading when we find her landing in Europe as Lola Montez, a stage dancer, and ending up as the royal mistress of King Ludwig I of Bavaria.

Lola Montez, Countess of Landsfeld (engraving by L.H. Garnier, c. 1835)

Born in 1818 at Lunmerick in Ireland, the daughter of a British military man, Lola Montez was baptized Maria Dolares Elisa Rosanna, a name pointing to her mother's Spanish origin. She was equally proud of her fiery Spanish temperament and her fine British traits, which enabled her to look younger and fresher than other Spanish women. She ran away in 1837 to avoid marrying an old man, Sir Abraham Lumley, and married Captain Thomas James, who was fifteen years older than she was and with whom she came to India.

The couple was invited to Simla to stay with her mother. A remarkably beautiful young woman, Mrs James became the focus of stares and gossip all over Simla, the imperial town known for its rounds of lively parties, romantic escapades, riding, and sports. Those days, Simla was notorious for its 'bright ladies', who outnumbered men and made the place an exciting resort for philandering and frivolity. No wonder, Mrs James attracted such great attention from all quarters, including the Governor General, whose sister Emily Eden 'found her undoubtedly very pretty and such a merry, unaffected girl' and even invited her to spend a day with her at the official camp in Karnal.

Not finding great prospects of name and fame in India, Mrs James returned to England in 1842 where her husband divorced her for having committed adultery during their journey home. She became a stage dancer and assumed the name Lola Montez. She had little success in England but won some fame in the European capitals of Paris, Berlin, Vienna, and Warsaw. She had utmost faith in her marvellous beauty and her seductive ways of influencing men. For her career as an international adventurer, she found her knowledge of several languages—English, French, and Spanish—extremely valuable and effective. She dressed with great elegance and skill. In fact, her sensual beauty and charm and her passionate affairs and scandals were talked about more than her art as a dancer which indeed was average.

Lola was welcomed and feted everywhere in Europe. Politicians, artists, writers, and poets—whomever she decided to please could not resist her unearthly spell.

'Lola's beauty,' says a contemporary writer, 'particularly the splendour of her breasts, made madmen everywhere.' A Polish paper, the *Warsaw Courier*, published the following eulogy to her beauty when she gave a performance at Warsaw in 1845:

The Spanish poet considers that a lovely woman should have the following twenty-seven beauties—three white:

the skin, the teeth, and the hands; three black: the eyes, the lashes, and the brows; three red; the lips, the cheeks, and the nails; three long: the body, the hair, and the hands; three short; the teeth, the ears, and the legs; three large: the breasts, the forehead, and the space between the two eyebrows; three slender: the waist, the hands, and the feet; three plump: the arms, the hips, and the thighs; three thin: the fingers, the hair, and the lips. All those attractions are possessed by Lola in perfect proportions, with the exception of the colour of her eyes—a circumstance which I consider the crown of her other charms. Hair soft as silk, rivalling the shining plumage of a raven falls luxuriantly down her back; on her slender, delicate neck, whose gleaming whiteness puts swans to shame, is poised her lovely face. How am I to describe even her teeth? So that the weakness of my pen may not diminish the fullness of truth, I must don borrowed plumes. Marino says of the goddess of love in the 78th stanza of the 8th Canto of Adone: 'On her lovely cheeks sweet flames of roses and rubies glowed, and in her bosom two perfect apples trembled in a milky sea.' Lola's little feet hold the mean between the daintiest Parisienne's and those of a Chinese woman; her lovely delicate calves are like the two lowest steps of a Jacob's ladder leading to heaven; . . . the greatest beauty of Lola, as of all women, her eyes were a deep forget-me-not blue.

Lola was an adventurer nonpareill, a fille de joie who is born and not made. Sexual desire played little part in her sport of seducing the high and mighty and climbing the ladder of fame and fortune. She would utilize her sex as a coin to secure adventure and excitement.

Lola had admirers wherever she displayed her seductive charm and beauty. She even captivated the famous composer and piano virtuoso Franz Liszt and accompanied him on many of his concert tours until she got tired of him and parted from him because he ceased to be useful to her. In Paris, she would count among her admirers Theophile Gautier, Alexander Dumas, Janin, Dujarier and other poets and writers. Dujarier was so infatuated with her that he picked up a fight with one of the critics who spoke against Lola and it ended in a duel.

Dujarier was unfortunately killed by his opponent and Lola had to leave Paris. She turned towards Germany where her reputation had already preceded her. She created a sensation when she arrived in Baden-Baden in 1846. She exhibited not only her physical beauty and graces but also her highly expensive dresses and jewels. Soon enough, she managed to win over King Henry LXXII of Reuss-Lobenstein Ebersdorf. She was excited about having a prince—though of a pocket royalty—as a lover, for hitherto she had succeeded only with bankers, merchants, artists, writers, and poets.

When she went with her lover to his tiny kingdom, her foreign appearance and arrogant bearing shocked the simple folk of the small capital. It was not long before her rough and sadistic actions offended the people of Reuss and the king's officers complained to their monarch. Even the lovelorn prince was shocked at Lola's misconduct, and calling her a 'female devil', banished her from his principality. The great adventurer, however, did not get disheartened over this sad episode; it only strengthened her determination to reach higher goals. Her astounding success with the rich and famous revived her confidence, and she managed to extract a fairly large sum from King Henry before her departure for Munich where she was destined to find the man she was looking for.

Every encounter with men of wealth and power enriched her experience of employing the irresistible feminine attraction to her advantage. She explored various ways and means to advance the fabulous art of seduction and pleasing men in the manner they wanted to be pleased. She knew how to bring a man completely under her sway with her voluptuous tenderness, her lively and ready wit, her remarkable high spirits and her instinctive talent of yielding to a man's advances at the most opportune moment. No wonder, she thrived and enjoyed playing with men who were led to believe that in Lola they had finally found a woman who could give them supreme rapturous love.

By the time Lola arrived in Munich in 1848, gossip columns of newspapers in Europe had already carried tales of her beauty, extravagances and discarded lovers, but very little about her success as a dancer on stage. So when she was refused an engagement by the Munich Theatre, she planned to do something spectacular. With absolute confidence in her irresistible beauty and instinctive knowledge of influencing men, she, without ceremony, marched straight to King Ludwig I whose numerous love affairs were well known to her. When denied entry at the palace, she raised a hue and cry, which attracted the attention of a senior palace official who got so fascinated by her beauty that he diplomatically persuaded his lord to receive the young dancer.

The sixty-year-old king was overwhelmed on seeing her in a closely fitting dress setting off her figure to perfection, particularly the alluring curves of her breasts. Noticing the king's amazement, and his misgivings about whether the beauty of her bosom was actually real, Lola, her vanity hurt by the unsaid suspicions, picked up a pair of scissors and swiftly slit open her dress, exposing the splendour. This bold and passionate gesture completely captivated the king and she rejoiced over her victory with a reassurance that the elderly roué would do everything she wanted. It was not long before the king got her a lovely little palace furnished with the greatest luxury to live in Munich.

He gladly went out of his way to satisfy her every whim and caprice. He was elated with his ageing senses being rejuvenated by the voluptuous beauty of a passionate mistress. This encouraged Lola to even interfere in the country's politics, to the annoyance of the citizens of Munich. Also her rough and arrogant behaviour agitated the local gentry who were greatly incensed with the king's mistress. She considered herself an autocrat and had no qualms about buying expensive dresses, jewellery and other gifts at Munich shops—all in the account of Le Roi. She signed her letters to business folk and officials as *Matiresse Du Roi*. She was provided with her own box at the theatre next to the royal box in the centre. King Ludwig was so deeply attached to Lola that he was even inspired to express his feelings in verses such as:

> Never thou grievest thy lover with heartless and idle caprices;
> Never with him dost thou play a wantoning game.
> Self-seeking knowest thou not; generous and kind is thy nature;
> Bounteous thou art, my Beloved, and ever the same.
> Happy is he who commands thy heart for his eager possessing!
> Not like those lovers who pine for a mistress unkind.
> Thou lovest, and love is for thee a bright and unquenchable beacon;
> Constant till death is thy heart, unaltered thy mind.

> Hunger and thirst of my soul, unquenched by Italian
> caresses—
> I thought to find happiness so, but found only pain—
> 'Happiness, happiness,' still I cried with insatiable
> longing,
> And such I discovered in thee, thou woman of Spain.

It was not only the king who was enchanted by the beautiful dancer. She had admirers in Munich both young and old who wore tiepins and carried cigarette cases and tobacco boxes adorned with her pictures. Lola delighted in leading an open life and kept her windows without shutters and curtains so that her ordinary admirers might look into the brightly lit rooms and observe her existence as a public performance. Her visitors, flirtations, and dressmakers fitting dresses on her naked body were all open to public gaze. Fuchs, a German writer, called her 'provocation incarnate' and describes her most aptly in these words:

> 'I am lust,' said her body. 'My breasts yearn for a lover's caressing hand; my limbs desire to stretch and tighten themselves in unbridled and eternal lust.' Her body sang this song in fascinating rhythm.

Lola employed all her skills to display her sensual beauty to provoke and attract men who found in her the incarnation of the eternal form of passion. She almost perfected the art of dressing herself so as to appear in a man's imagination naked; she wore closely fitting riding clothes to exhibit better the undulations of her bosom and inert movements of her thighs, producing an effect of nakedness without showing anything. Everything about her provoked desire; her every gesture promised pleasure. She raised her eroticism almost to the level of a work of art.

The bourgeois classes of Munich with their noble concepts of morality and decency were horrified with Lola who seemed lust incarnate. At the same time, her arrogant and callous behaviour and utter disrespect for law and justice brought scorn from the people, earning her the title of 'devil woman'. Despite her great influence over the king, who did everything she wanted, Lola never succeeded in winning a place in aristocratic society. Many luminaries of high society kept their contacts with the royal mistress a secret for the sake of appearances. Eventually, she went too far and there was a great hue and cry against the royal favourite, who was held responsible for all the king's faults. To overcome the popular clamour, the king removed his eccentric mistress from the scene and sent her to Weinsberg to a mesmerist for 'driving the devil out of her', as she was said to be possessed. Lola did not submit to the 'devil cure' and managed to return to Munich, but King Ludwig dismissed her.

Lola went to England in 1849 and got married to George Trafford Heald, but was prosecuted for bigamy since her earlier marriage with Captain Thomas James had not been legally dissolved. She escaped with her husband George to Spain where he died in 1853. Later, she went to New York to pursue her career as a stage dancer and married P.P. Hull, a rich American. But she left him, and then in 1859 she met an old schoolfellow who influenced her to follow the path of religion. She died in 1861 while engaged in charitable services for fallen women.

7

Corruption, Scandal and Gossip

Contemporary Raj literature includes many stories of rampant corruption among the John Company's officials who were more interested in their own private trade at the expense of the Company's profits. A number of early English settlers were desperate adventurers, bent on amassing fortunes through any means, fair or foul. The state of morals in eighteenth-century Calcutta was so low that the city was described by Clive as:

> . . . one of the most wicked Places in the Universe. Corruption, Licentiousness and a want of Principle seem to have possessed the Minds of all the Civil servants. By frequent bad examples they have grown callous, Rapacious and Luxurious beyond Conception and the incapacity and iniquity of some and the Youth of others . . .

It was here that the British nabobs flourished and then returned home with vast fortunes to acquire social status and prestige and in some cases even to buy out seats in the Parliament. Ridiculed as loathsome upstarts and even plunderers, these nabobs with their ostentatious lifestyle were the butt of jokes and a popular subject for caricaturists.

The Company's soldiers did not lag behind in this game of money. They extracted money from the nawabs engaged in the play of musical crowns and also from wealthy zamindars in return for giving them the Company's protection. After Plassey, presents worth £1.24 million were distributed to various Englishmen, and Clive himself received the equivalent of £234,000. In 1763, following the defeat of Mir Kasim, the total amount paid to the English 'in restitution' amounted to about £4 million but it was reported that the Company received only half a million. No wonder, this ill-gotten wealth led Company officials to heavy drinking, gambling and revelling in all kinds of vices. During Warren Hastings's time, it was not uncommon for English officers to sit over their cups until death came to claim one of the revellers. Gambling parties would begin on Saturday and carried on well into the following week. Francis, a member of the Council, once won at a single sitting £20,000, and on another occasion Barwell lost £40,000.

This was the golden age of corruption, when bribery thrived both in India as well as in England. In an interesting case recorded in his famous memoirs, William Hickey, an eminent attorney of Calcutta, refers to one Col. Auchmuty who openly admitted that he gave Company directors in London 5,000 guineas for the appointment of his two sons in Calcutta and got a cadetship for his third son in the Company's army in the bargain. Patronage played an important part in the Company service; the recruits were the sons or close relations of the directors and these connections tended to be hereditary. The pursuit of wealth was the only attraction that brought them to the land of 'broiling sun and scorching wind'. There were also other dubious ways of entering the Company's employment. Notices appeared in the London newspapers during the second half of the eighteenth century advertising writerships in the Company for as much as £2,000 or £3,000. The temptation was not the salary, which was nominal, as the first entrant joined as a writer with an annual salary of £5, rising to £15 as a factor, followed by £30 for a junior merchant and £40 for a senior one, and the governors at presidency towns received a salary of £300 per annum. These ridiculously low salaries were supplemented by private trade and gifts from the native rulers and aristocracy.

To return to the prevalent corruption—Capt. Hamilton, a shipowner who visited Calcutta regularly, recounts an exceptionally amazing case of a seaman's pretty Eurasian wife prone to amorous ways during her husband's absences. She had two Armenian lovers who began quarrelling about sharing her favours. When told about it, the governor reprimanded the lovers. However, when one of them bribed the governor, he was awarded with the sole right to her attentions. He took her home, praising the governor for this deal. When the husband returned from the sea, he was forced to submit to the governor's orders. There were very few who opposed the most blatant forms of bribery. So much so that Governor General Hastings once made up his mind to end the squabble with his opponents in the Council by buying them up, £100,000 a piece. Clive, vexed by the unruly, incompetent officials put in comfortable berths in the Company through influential contacts, had even suggested buying them out as soon as they landed in Calcutta. An amusing picture of the state of affairs published in the *Calcutta Gazette* (1780) is described as follows:

What is commerce? Gambling.
What is the most cardinal virtue? Riches.
What's the Amor Patriae? Amor Sui.
What is fraud? Detection.
What is beauty? Paint.
What is punctuality? An observance of the appointments
of duelling and intriguing.
What is gentility? Extravagance.
What are public taxes? Pack saddles.
Who are the people? Nobody.

The English mercantile morality in eighteenth century
was no better and had quite a poor reputation. The
only aim was to make quick fortune, and dishonesty
was the driving force whether it was Company's business
or private trade. Atkinson in his 'City of Palaces' thus
alludes to this state of things:

Calcutta! Nurse of opulence and vice,
Thou architect of European fame
And fortune, fancied beyond earthly price,
Envy of sovereigns, and constant aim
Of kin adventurers, art thou not the same
As other sinks where manhood rots in state?
Sparkling with phosper brightness—
There stood proud cities once, of ancient date,
Close parallels to thee, denounced by angry fate.

Civilian morality was no higher. According to an enquiry
into the conduct of civilians, the report to the court in
1765 noted:

Their transactions seem to demonstrate that every
spring of the Government was smeared with corruption,
that principles of rapacity and oppression universally
prevailed, that every spark and sentiment of public
spirit was lost and extinguished in the abandoned lust
of universal wealth. The residences of Europeans and

free merchants away from the Presidency had frequently given birth to acts of insult and oppression.

The Company directors in London endeavoured to check corruption and one Governor Weldon was even sacked for accepting bribes through his wife and daughter. The Company officials on the other hand defended themselves by asserting that presents or gifts were offered as per established custom of Mughal life. They were voluntary offerings for certain services done in the course of duty and did not in any way adversely affect the Company's interest. A lakh of rupees (£11,000) was a standard present from a Mughal ruler. It was the 'Age of Nabobs', a mad world of luxury and fortune-hunting. Clive made some efforts to curb some of the worst abuses and Warren Hastings continued the process of reform but it was the British Parliament's Regulating Act of 1774 and the steep rise in salaries of Company officials that brought discipline in Company's affairs during Lord Cornwallis's regime (1786–93). This Act and subsequent measures adopted by Lord Wellesley (1798–1805) laid the formal foundation of the British Empire in India, with Calcutta as the imperial capital of all the territories under the Company's rule.

As regards the practice of religion, this was at a low ebb in eighteenth-century Calcutta. It was wittingly observed that on their way to India, Englishmen dropped their religion at the Cape and forgot to take it up again on their return home. According to Alexander Hamilton's account, Company officials decided after viewing a number of Portuguese Catholic churches in Bombay to build a Protestant church of 'form proportionable to the small churches in England so that the heathen should observe the purity and gravity of our doctrines'. A sum of £5,000 was collected through voluntary contributions by the Company's servants. But there was no sign of any church as the entire amount was embezzled by Governor Sir John Child.

According to Sir Charles Raikes, the only evidence of Sundays was the flag hoisted in cantonments. Ladies worked, men played cards. Occasionally, a spinster might be found to boast that she read over the Church Service on Sundays whilst her ayah was combing her hair. The first church in Calcutta was consecrated in 1787. Earlier, Sunday services were held at the Custom House. Until the beginning of the nineteenth century, missionaries were considered a dangerous class of men not conducive to the Company's economic and political aims and ambitions. They were prohibited from public preaching in the native language in Calcutta. It was reckoned unfashionable to attend church. As the story goes, Lord Wellesley halting at a civil station on one Sunday requested the judge to read the Church Service but was informed there would be some difficulty as there was no copy of the Bible available with anyone at the station. No wonder, young Company servants got influenced by native customs and rituals. So much so that there was one army officer who gladly agreed to be circumcised in order to get possession of a young pretty Muslim maiden who insisted on his circumcision before submitting to be his mistress.

When the John Company copied the Portuguese practice and shipped some Englishwomen for marriage with their officials, it was found that some women took to prostitution as a more lucrative and agreeable vocation than marriage. There was another amusing case of one Miss Ward of this group who had £3,000 of her own. The Bombay governor, Sir John Gayor, succeeded in marrying her to his son after declaring her earlier marriage to a Company employee as void. Later, she was found having an illicit affair with a schoolmaster who was arrested and sent home in chains.

As the nineteenth century wore on, the irregular unions of sahibs with Indian women were frowned upon. Then came the 'Age of Memsahibs', which meant the banishment of the bibi and the downfall of the Eurasian, or half-caste. Here is a description of the birth of Qui Hi's son in the satiric poem 'The Grand Master' (1816):

> Poor *Gaulaub* now was in *that* way,
> That those 'who love their lords,' should be;
> And in a week, to QUI HI's joy,
> Produced our youth a chopping boy.
> The deuce! said Qui HI, with a curse;
> It's well, however, it's no worse;
> For what the d—I could he do,
> If he had *manufactur'd* two,
> Like other ladies, that he knew.
> Our hero now, without pretence,
> Thought himself of *some consequence;*
> A child he'd got, and what was curious.
> He knew the infant was not spurious;
> For tho' QUI HI was never tied
> By *licence* to his Indian bride,
> Yet he was confident that she
> Had acted with fidelity.
> How many husbands, to their shame,
> Would hesitate to say the same;——
> But now he finds he must submit,
> To European damsels wit;
> Wherever QUI HI did appear,
> The spinsters titter, chat, and jeer.

'O dear, Miss *Pinchback,* have you heard,
'La! what a scandal—on my word;'
'What,' (said Miss Pinchback) 'prithe say?
'Tell us the scandal of the day?'
'The fellow! but we'll send him out
'Of our society, no doubt;
'There's sweet Miss *Wababina Stocking,*
'*She* can repeat it—'*tis so shocking;*
'That QUI HI's *creature,* it is said,
'The other day was brought to bed.'
'Oh heaven!' exclaimed Miss Indigo,
'And could he then have *us'd* me so?
'And with a *black one* too connected,

. . .

'A precious precedent's begun,
'A mistress first, and then a son.'

We owe to some women writers the prevalence of gossip in the presidency towns of Calcutta, Bombay and Madras. Most memsahibs with an army of servants had abundant leisure and their chief occupation was of course gossip. Whenever they heard a fresh piece of news, they could not contain themselves and hurriedly sent out chits to their friends. It was said that on an average, a socialite lady sent twenty-five chits every day. In other parts of the world people talked about things but here they talked about people. The conversation was all personal—what Mr This said to Miss That, and what Miss That did to Mr This, and then all the gossip about marriages, elopements, scandalous affairs and ladies flirtings.

According to Lady Falkland, the newly arrived damsels at Calcutta or Bombay were hot topics of conversation, and their age, height, features, dress and manners came under scrutiny and also their prospects of procuring husbands. Mrs Elwood described Scandal Point at Breach Candy in Bombay where the memsahibs gathered to discuss the affairs of the day:

> Who danced with whom and who is likely to wed,
> And who is hanged and who is brought to bed; . . .

They would sit there for an hour at a time talking about their neighbours and killing reputations. Dr Howson says:

> . . . were the Genius of Scandals at a loss where to establish his headquarters he would recommend that their site should be at Bombay . . . for in no other part of the world where he has ever been is the propensity of gossiping so unintermitting.

That may be one version but Calcutta or Madras did not lag behind. The *Calcutta Gazette* (1820) speaks about a 'Raffle for Ladies'. As the memsahibs turned up to hunt for husbands, the demand was much greater than the supply. A very amusing advertisement called 'A raffle for ladies' was reported to have appeared in the *Madras Journal*, announcing that on a certain day a number of females recently imported would be put into a sort of lottery. In a letter to the editor of the *Calcutta Gazette*, one of the readers commented that the most fortunate holder of lottery tickets would have the first choice out of the collection. He added, 'whether any of the tickets of this lottery or raffle were divided or shared we do not learn; but if they were it is difficult to see how the matter could be adjusted: for suppose one female to fall to the lot of two, three or four gentlemen, in what way could the business be settled unless the gentlemen again threw among themselves for the lucky chance or unless they consented to stated periods of possession which if the practice of raffling be allowed at all, is not impossible.'

There was also a lot of gossip about the spinsters in Calcutta. By the third decade of the nineteenth century, with introduction of the overland route and steamships, an increasing number of memsahibs began arriving in India in search of rich husbands. But by now there was little scope of making quick fortunes, which meant that many damsels failed in their search of the riches they were looking for. This led to a growing number of spinsters in Calcutta who thereupon set up a Spinsters' Secret Society to enquire into the cause of the infrequency of marriages and explore ways and means to win over eligible bachelors and prevent encroachments by some discontented wives who had poached on the preserves which the spinsters considered their exclusive game. The activities of the Spinsters' Society prompted the bachelors of Calcutta to form a Jawaub Club whose members had made marriage proposals but were rejected or *jawaub*ed. The objective was that disappointed would-be lovers have consolation and sympathy from others who had suffered a similar fate.

Another topic of gossip was the extramarital adventures of some wives when they were left behind at home. The popular expression was *darwaza-bund* (the door is shut) to which several meanings were attached by the visitors. As per contemporary records it was interpreted as follows:

> In some instances it implies that the lady of the house is lazy, and has not dressed to receive visitors, in others that lady is ill, or perhaps otherwise occupied, and that she is attending on it: on some occasions, that she is suffering from one or other of the numerous forms of

indisposition that afflict the sex in India. All these are valid excuses in their way; but how comes it that at such and such a house where we received this message, we saw, standing in the compound, a buggy and horse extremely like those of Captain Snooks, of one of the native regiments that after four years' residence at the station mutinied and dissolved themselves? How can we reconcile this little fact with the message we have just received? The interpretation is, however, easy. It signifies that the lady is more agreeably occupied than she would be if receiving us.

The medical profession also became a butt of jokes and the doctors were ill-equipped to treat common diseases. There was race between the doctor and the disease as to which would kill the patient first. Whatever the ailment, the patient preferred the therapeutic value of Claret which he consumed in large quantities to alleviate the suffering. A humorous verse published in the *Bengal Gazette* (1781) throws light on the contemporary state of affairs.

> Some doctors in India would make Plato smile
> If you fracture your skull they pronounce it the bile
> A sprain in your toe or an anguish shiver
> The faculty here call a touch of liver.

8

When Sahib was Hooked to Hookah

When the British came as traders, the Mughals and their Persian culture dominated the Indian scene. The early settlers were greatly influenced by the Indian lifestyle and adopted local customs and habits in respect of food and dress. There was no colour prejudice and marriages with native women were common and even encouraged by the East India Company. In the field of recreation and amusement, the British became more Indianized as we find them riding out for shikar, enjoying nautch parties, playing chess, and smoking the hookah. In fact they tried to adopt any Indian fashion or custom which made life more delicious and enjoyable.

The Indian hookah is described as an elegant and expensive equipage of a very complex form consisting of five individual components: the hookah bottom serving as a water reservoir, a snake or tube, a mouthpiece, an earthen chillum and a silver cover which fitted the rim of the chillum. The pleasure of hookah smoking seems to have found favour with some early English merchants as references to the hookah can be found in the *Factory*

Miscellaneous Records of 1675. Company inventories too reveal the dominance of the hookah.

Hookah smoking thus became a favourite pastime by the middle of the eighteenth century and contemporary Raj literature carries interesting information about this

An hookaburdar (by B. Solvyns, c. 1790)

luxurious habit which required an employment of a special servant, the hookahburdar, whose duty it was to be in readiness with his master's hookah and all its accompaniments in perfect order whenever he may be called for, and particularly after meals.

When dinner was removed, the hookahburdar entered the room with the prepared and lighted hookah which he placed behind his master's chair on a small mat or stand, presented him with the snake (flexible tube), and with a phial of rose water from his girdle, a small quantity of which, poured through the mouth piece, imparted additional freshness to the smoke of the chillum as it passed through. He then took his station behind the hookah which he attentively watched and kept in order with his tongs, taking care also in due time to prepare a fresh chillum, and when his master said, 'doosra chillum lao' (bring another chillum), to be quick in replacing the old one with it.

The most unpleasant element of the hookah was the loud rattling of water, caused by the quick passage of the tobacco smoke through it. In large parties this produced a loud concert of violent snoring noises.

The popularity of the hookah extended even to the Governor General's palace at Calcutta as seen from the following invitation issued from the Government House in 1779:

> Mr and Mrs Hastings present their compliments to Mr . . . and request the favour of his company to a concert and supper on Thursday next. Mr . . . is requested to bring no servants except his hookah-burdar.

This invitation also shows that even the first lady of Calcutta was indulgent to the practice of hookah smoking. The fashion of hookah smoking was so well established that even memsahibs had got addicted to it. The nautch, rice pullao and curry, chewing of pan and the hookah were all part of the same culture.

Grand Pre, a French traveller who visited Calcutta in 1789 gives the following account in his journal:

> Every *hookahburdar* prepares separately that of his master in an adjoining apartment and entering all together with the dessert they range themselves round the table. For half an hour there is a continued glamour, and nothing is distinctly heard but the cry for silence, till the noise subsides and the conversation assumes its usual tone. It is scarcely possible to see through the cloud of smoke, which fills the apartment. The effect produced by these circumstances is whimsical enough to a stranger and if he has not his hookah he will find himself in an awkward and unpleasant situation. The rage of smoking extends even to the ladies, and the highest compliment they can pay a man is to give him preference by smoking his hookah. In this case it is a point of politeness to take off a mouthpiece he is using and substitute a fresh one, which he presents to the lady with his hookah who soon returns it. This compliment is not always of trivial importance, it sometimes signifies a great deal to a friend, and often still more to a husband.

At formal dinners, the hookahs were placed before the invited guests. Stavorinus writes about a dinner given to a Dutch director in Bengal when silver hookahs were placed before each director of the Company. The luxury of hookah smoking consisted not only in the fine quality and frequent washings of the tobacco, but also mixing with it dried fruits, the conserve of roses, sweet herbs, spices, and a variety of fragrant ingredients. The sweet-smelling smoke was then inhaled from the snake eight or ten feet in length and drawn through the rose water in the hookah bottom, which remained at a pleasant temperature.

The British nabobs of the day watched nautches and enjoyed Persian poetry while the hookah snakes encircled their waists as they puffed through the gold or ivory mouthpieces.

The hookah was considered not only fashionable but also an indispensable article in the dining room of every house of affluent and respectable sahibs. Also, the hookah rug was considered a fancy carpet piece, often presented to friends and relatives on special occasions. Hookahs added glamour to dinner parties when they were brought in at a specified time. One could then witness sometimes thirty hookahs on each side of the table, one behind almost every diner. The gargle of these sixty hookahs would produce a strange and rather discordant music, but no dinner would have been rated complete and elegant without these grand hookahs.

The exotic cloudy scene is aptly described in the following lines composed by a contemporary resident of Calcutta:

> What is it through halls magnificently long
> Rolls the thick clouds and tunes the hollow song,
> 'Tis thou O Hookah! source of calm delight!
> Oft grasped at morn, and played upon till night.

The ultimate luxury of smoking the hookah was to take its puffs while enjoying palanquin travel, the most popular mode of conveyance in those days. As the bearers carried their master in the palanquin, the hookahburdar would run alongside carrying the hookah in full operation.

The etiquette of smoking a hookah in those days demanded that one should never step over another's hookah snake. It was considered a great insult and many duels were fought over it to save the hookah's honour.

The wealthy sahibs' fancy for their hookahs inspired them to have their hookah bottoms made of silver and gold studded with precious stones, with their own monograms. Also available were beautiful cut-glass hookah bottoms of British manufacture, but the most common were of black metal inlaid with silver. The snake was composed of a light brass or silverware spirally twisted and then finished with a covering of fine silk or brocade ornamented with gold or silver at the head and tail. The mouthpiece was a symbol of one's wealth and so was made either of solid gold, silver, agate or ivory. The tobacco mixture was also specially prepared by adding dried fruits, conserve of roses, and a variety of fragrant ingredients, and then matured by keeping it underground in earthen jars for a few weeks.

The hookahs were of different designs and names. In Bombay, hookahs were known as 'Cream Cans', apparently named after Karim Khan Zend, the king of South Persia who had reportedly invented it. Another type was the 'Ailoon', which was also of Persian origin. The poor man's hookah was called the hubble-bubble. Another variety is mentioned as the 'Kalian',—a Western hookah with a large bottom. In Surat, hookahs were called 'Nargils' and in Calcutta a small hookah used by common folk was called 'gargara'. It was, however, in Lucknow and in the other princely states of Rajasthan that the hookah was seen in all its splendour and with every embellishment.

Hookah smoking was universal among the sahibs and memsahibs of Bombay and Calcutta. Emily Eden, sister of Governor General Auckland, noted in 1837, 'aide-de-camps and doctors get their newspapers and hookah' in the morning.

But later, as the nineteenth century rolled on, hookah smoking began to decline. A hookah was more expensive than a cigar or a pipe because besides the cost of rose water and tobacco it also required a special servant to service it. The new arrivals found it an expensive luxury, which not many of them could easily afford. So hookah smoking fell into bad days, and Sir Charles D'Oyley in *The European in India* notes that not one in three were then smokers although the custom had been almost universal. Later there were opponents of the custom who condemned hookah smoking in the columns of the Calcutta press, but the custom did not go away so easily and it came to light that some old gentlemen took their hookahs to England and one lady is said to have used it in Scotland for many years.

The custom vanished in the presidency towns, but it lingered on in other parts of the country until the middle of the nineteenth century when it was replaced by the cheroot and the cigar.

9

From Arrack to Wine and Whisky

Among the early English settlers, everyone from the governors to factors and soldiers enjoyed drinks and many of them were addicted to excessive drinking. Alcohol provided an escape from boredom and loneliness and helped to stimulate their spirits and general attitude towards life. Even at the beginning of the seventeenth century Sir Thomas Roe found frequent bouts of drunkenness at most English tables. Drinking was considered one of the 'rational amusements' with which they sought to beguile time, with the income of the drinker determining not only the quantity but also the quality of the drink.

The most popular and staple drink in the early days was arrack, a term applied to a variety of common spirits. French traveller Bernier was surprised at the English liking for arrack, which he considered very hot and penetrating like Polish brandy, made from corn. Of the two principal brands of arrack, the one from Bengal was stronger while the other from Goa, though of better quality, was comparatively milder and was both drunk and used for making yeast. Captain Symson, an authority on the subject, describes different kinds and uses of arrack (1720): 'It was distilled sometimes from rice, sometimes from toddy and sometimes from black sugar and water mixed with the bark of a tree called "Baboul", when it was known as "Jagre Arrack" and was as hot as brandy and drunk in drams by Europeans.'

Arrack was also credited with some medicinal properties. It was said to be good for gripes, in the morning as laxative, in the evening as astringent. But Symson added that several Europeans 'lose their lives by the immoderate use of arrack with which once inflamed they become so restless that no place is cool enough; and therefore they lie down on the ground all night which occasions their being snatched away in a very short time.'

Arrack formed the basis of punch, a word derived from the Persian panj or Hindi panch, both meaning five. Arrack also got its name from the number of its ingredients: arrack, sugar, lime juice, spice, and water. This was easily the most popular drink and became a universal favourite in the first half of the eighteenth century. The popularity of arrack was also attributed to the fact that it could be preserved and stored through even the hottest weather, which was not the case with wines imported from Europe. It was common for everyone to consume large quantities of punch and even Company members of the Council did so in their morning meetings regularly. Historian Cotton writes; 'We may picture them, dressed in muslin shirts, pyjamas, and starched white caps sitting—with a case of good old Arrack and a goblet of water on the table—which the secretary with a skilful hand converted into punch.' An English captain Farwinter of Bengal Masonic Lodge liked arrack so much that he sent a chest of the best arrack for the use of the Grand Lodge in England. It was punch that gave its name to the Portuguese drinking taverns, which came to be called punch houses.

In those early hard-drinking years, sailors and soldiers were known for their reckless drinking which swallowed most of their pay. It was even reported that captains of ships run by the East India Company made their crew drunk with liquors they trafficked in. Drunkenness was common according to early Company records of Bombay as well. Not only soldiers, but even officers drank excessively.

There was a shocking case of one Captain Wyatt who in a drunken rage murdered a soldier with his sword, but the Company was so indulgent that they just sacked him, considering it as sufficient punishment for a gentleman. Many soldiers drank strong Portugal wines at the hottest time of the day. No wonder a number of them died of intemperance. Another ruinous drink was hot wine boiled with cloves and cinnamon, called burnt wine. Soldiers drank it frequently in the mornings to comfort their stomachs. They did not suspect any connection between drinking and high mortality rates.

Eighteenth-century doctors considered wine an antidote to fever in hot weather if taken in the right quantity. In Madras, alcohol was considered necessary for soldiers to counteract the ill effects of the bad water they drank. It was also thought to be useful in enhancing the fighting spirit of the soldiers. They were given an extra allowance of arrack before they went into action and were ordered to drink it up on the day of issue. No wonder there was a contemporary saying that 'people's lives were not worth two monsoons'. Once, in Calcutta, an arrack licence was withdrawn from a Mr Hundle because military men of the Company were found 'continually intoxicated with liquor in his tavern'.

The difficulty of growing grapes in India was an obstacle in making local wine. The East India Company later imported Shiraz wine from Persia, which was much in favour. Mr Ives writes about this (1757) saying that Shiraz was supplied by the Company to its servants at the western factories and was the best he ever tasted except claret. Towards the close of the eighteenth century, European wines were being imported for those who could afford to pay the high prices fixed for them. Moreover, punch and arrack became less popular and gave way to Madeira and later to claret and beer.

There was also a gradual realization that it was better to live than to drink oneself to an untimely grave. Mr Tennant recorded in 1796 that 'regularity of living and temperance are much more prevalent among the present inhabitants than the first adventurers'. Madeira wine was now the most popular drink. So much so that one advertiser (1790) announced the arrival of his new stock of Madeira with the following couplet:

Now drink Madeira and in scorn of knaves
Leave continental wines to conquered slaves.

Large shipments of wines from England and France were now regularly arriving in Calcutta. Even the Company did a little business in Madeira. It imported a large quantity annually for the use of its servants and any surplus was sold to the public. The wine was then stored and kept by the same buyers for later sale at high profit. The favourite Madeira was said to improve in the Indian climate and it was a common practice to drink Madeira before dinner and claret with dinner and afterwards when the gentlemen would sit down to relax and easily polish off three bottles each. For ladies it was common to drink at least a bottle while some of them competed with men in the consumption of booze. Captain Edouard de Warren, a Frenchman who served for nine years in a British regiment in India, recorded in his book *L'Inde Anglaise* (1843) his surprise at the enormous quantity of beer and wine consumed by English women. He speaks about a lady at a dinner party who calmly put down a bottle and a half of very strong beer, alternately with a certain amount of burgundy, and finished up with five or six glasses of champagne. The only effect this had on her was to loosen her tongue and give vivacity to her eyes.

It is interesting to note the prices of wines and spirits from contemporary advertisements in the early nineteenth

Drinking session, Bombay (by Rowlandson, c. 1840)

century. Madeira wine was priced at Rs 40 for a dozen bottles (sixteen years old) and Rs 28 for a dozen (for seven-year-old wines). Red sparkling champagne was sold at Rs 45 for a dozen, white at Rs 40, port wine at Rs 25, gin at Rs 15, pale ale at Rs 11 and brandy at Rs 16. Around this time, soda water was also introduced in Calcutta, substituting the use of soda powder. It was proclaimed as a pleasant drink and a valuable remedy for indigestion, comparable in quality to that made in London. Soda water was found useful for diluting strong spirits like brandy, gin, and later whisky. Later, the importing of ice from America added another flavour to the enjoyment of drinking.

By the end of the nineteenth century a number of breweries were set up in different parts of India and locally produced beer, rum, gin, and whisky found their way to the market. Drinking habits and tastes of the native gentry were also transformed. Contemporary advertisements in the newspapers of metropolitan cities suggest a growing demand among the Indian gentry not only for whisky, rum, and gin, but also for exotic French wines, champagne, and cognac.

The dawn of the twentieth century saw the emergence of Scotch whisky as the first choice of the connoisseurs. It was a ritual for an Englishman to have his sundowner, whisky and soda on the veranda of his bungalow. The custom was attributed to the apprehension that sunset was particularly bad for catching malaria and a strong drink taken at that time was the best antidote.

There is no historical record of when and where the first cask of whisky was distilled in Scotland, but ancient Celts proclaimed it as the 'water of life'. Its popularity soared over the centuries and it was in the

1820s that the Scottish government legalized distilleries and the production of whisky. The great popularity of Scotch whisky is attributed to the traditional skill of the Scotsmen in maturing and blending of whisky, the quality of water and the oak barrels and even the structure of the warehouses. The skilful art of blending is highly complex as the master blender has to ensure that the individual elements produce a consistent aroma and taste in the finished brand of whisky. Originally praised for its medicinal properties, it is still accepted as a blood thinner and is believed to be good for the human heart.

After the First World War, there was a spurt in the popularity of whisky. It was hailed as an ideal drink for the Indian climate. It was a wonderful stimulant, and a small dose would accomplish more than what a few glasses of wine could. G.W. Osborne, who accompanied Governor General Auckland to Maharaja Ranjit Singh's court in 1838 gives a graphic account of the maharaja's colourful drinking parties and his special wine extracted from raisins and mixed with ground pearls. He points out that of all the European wines and spirits presented to him, whisky was the only drink Maharaja Ranjit Singh liked. The maharaja scoffed at European wines and said that he drank for excitement, and that the sooner that object was attained the better. No wonder, whisky, the queen of drinks, reigned supreme and is the most popular drink in the subcontinent.

10

Fun and Frolic in Simla

Among the notable contributions of the Raj are the hill stations opened up by the British in the nineteenth century. Simla was the pride of the Raj. It was Kipling's great and gay summer capital of India. Perched on a steep ridge 7,000 feet above sea level, it was also called Mount Olympus, the 'Indian Capua' and the 'abode of Hindu gods'. It provided escape from the searing heat of the plains, a refuge for the invalid and the bored, a fun place with escapades for the pleasure-seeker. Above all, with its pines and flowers in the misty landscape, it reminded Englishmen of home. Many considered it 'not really a part of India'.

Lord Amherst was the first Governor General who in 1827 started the custom of summering in Simla. It was far from easy to move to the hills. But Simla became popular nevertheless. More and more Englishmen and women went there. The atmosphere was relaxed. Snow-capped mountains were a balm. In 1819, a thatched wooden cottage was first put up by Lieutenant Ross, assistant political agent for the hill states. His successor, Captain Kennedy, built the first house in Simla in 1822. As time passed, the place was dotted with elegant villas like Swiss chalets standing amid flower gardens with English names on their gateways. There were thirty houses in 1830. The number rose to more than a hundred in 1841, and to 290 in 1866. By 1880, there were as many as 1,000 houses. The weather was considered 'good for the liver, good for the soul' and helped to protect the constitutions of those suffering from 'too much East' as was the saying of the times. Emily Eden, sister of the Governor General, Lord Auckland, was moved by the sights of Simla and said: 'Well, it really is worth all the trouble—such a beautiful place.'

Known for its round of lively parties, fetes and fairs, fancy dress balls, romantic escapades, riding and sports, Simla acquired a lasting reputation for 'bright ladies and gay gentlemen'. Women outnumbered men and had endless opportunities for casual flirtations. It was common practice for European women to share a house with another wife, or rent a flat while their husbands would visit them for a week or two. On the other hand, young civil or military officers on a holiday were on the loose. Ethel Savi noted that 'women were ready to make merry in mountains while their husbands toiled on the plains'. *The Delhi Sketchbook,* a sort of Indian *Punch,* commenting on why so many women really went to Simla every year wrote thus about the typical residents.

Good motherly Mrs A because her children's health requires it, and little flirtatious Mrs B, who had no children, because of her own did. Mrs C certainly lived at the dullest of outstations and everybody knew its weather half-killed her . . . Miss O went up because she was Miss O and did not wish to be so any longer, while Mrs L was determined that her daughters should not be long in the plains, so took them up the first season.

The presence of many grass widows and husband-hunters around made Simla popular with bachelors. It acquired a reputation as a resort for philandering and frivolity. It was a haunt of the gallant, the matchmaker, the chivalrous and the flirt. Dr Hoffmeister, who accompanied Prince Waldemar to Simla in 1845, wrote:

> . . . kind and thoughtful relatives at Simla never fail to bring up from the plains everything in the shape of young and marriageable nieces and cousins; and where so many agreeable officers are stationed for pleasure's sake alone, many a youthful pair are thrown together, and many a match is made.

Circumstances and ambience were an ideal mix for romance. The early Victorian Simla was as notorious for its scandals as in Kipling's day. Indeed, it became a resort, as the French traveller Victor Jacquemont put it, for the rich, the idle and the invalid.

In 1864, the viceroy, Lord John Lawrence, made Simla the official summer capital on strategic grounds and also for its advantageous location for receiving the

Arrival of the mail tonga at the post office (photograph, c. 1890)

great chiefs of northern and western India who came to Simla to pay their respects to the British suzerain. The whole viceregal machine began moving up there from Calcutta. The secretariat circles came to form the nucleus of Simla society. As the nineteenth century rolled on, and means of transport improved, Simla became increasingly crowded with summer visitors from military cantonments and wealthy business people of Calcutta. The place now also attracted officers who sought promotions, staff appointments or better prospects. For this goal, they tried to socialize with those in power and it was whispered that it paid to be useful to someone's wife or for one's wife to be useful to someone's husband. The gentlemen with their wives adopted novel methods of attracting attention. One lady reportedly made sketches of the Governor General in order to curry favour for her 'sad fool' of a husband. Another amateur artist sketched in full colour the C-in-C's favourite horse and the next Gazette announced the promotion of Capt. C as a major of brigade. A humorous verse 'Promotion' described the importance of Simla for achieving that goal:

> Had the psalmist a vision of Simla,
> When he sang of promotion of eld,
> Bidding votaries look to northward,
> 'Ere her fervour and form they beheld
>
> Was the session made of grass widows
> And of men of promotion all bent;
> And say who were the women who helped them,
> To gain their unselfish intent?
>
> O promotion! thou stern northern goddess!
> Thou art still quite hard to attain;
> And thy votaries who soar not to Simla
> Must look for thy favour in vain.

The tone was set by the viceroy and his lady. The Lyttons enjoyed holding balls and encouraged amateur dramatics. Critics called Simla 'wicked'. But Lord Lytton 'perhaps used to a higher level of wickedness' made fun of the public parade of piety in a letter to Lady Salisbury in 1876: 'I envy you the pleasure of living among so many naughty people—our social surroundings here are so grievously good . . . I believe the moonlight picnics were forbidden last year by order of the Governor General in Council lest they should lead to immorality.'

The Dufferins were fond of amusement. The fancy-dress ball held by them in 1887, Queen Victoria's golden jubilee year, was acclaimed as the most dazzling ever. At this ball Lord Dufferin amazed everyone with his disguise as an Arab gentleman and even his wife did not recognize him even when he spoke to her.

The main drawback was that with the shortage of men, women could not be invited to every official party. It was even rumoured that desperate ladies bribed clerks to procure invitations and some daring ones simply showed up at the gate, saying they had lost their invitations.

One of the delights of Simla was the public playground at Anandale. Named after a glen of the same name in Scotland or according to another story after the first lady called Anna who 'graced its solitude', the verdant valley surrounded by an amphitheatre of hills was described as 'a romantic glen, picturesque dell' where pleasure-seekers would bring their companions for dallying. It provided an ideal spot for fancy fairs, picnics, polo matches, horse and dog shows and race meetings. Dance parties were also organized in the cool evenings. A fancy fair held there during Emily Eden's time in 1839 was acclaimed for its splendour. It lasted twelve hours or so and most of Simla's European population took an active part in it. A turnpike gate with a canvas cottage was erected at the entrance, with a board announcing 'Charity Toll Bar' and one Capt. P, dressed as a funny old woman, collecting the dues. In 1845, Prince Waldemar of Prussia was given a royal send-off with a brilliant fête also held at Anandale.

Fun and frolic were the order of the day. The popular mode of transport for the ladies in the early nineteenth century was the *jampan*, a kind of sedan chair slung on poles carried by four porters called *jampanees*. By the 1880s a new device from Japan, known as the rickshaw, was introduced.

The Indian model with an adjustable hood as a protection against rain was hauled by four men who ran downhill ringing the bell and pulled it uphill with loud groans. Burrah (senior) memsahibs engaged their rickshaw-pullers for the season and dressed them in colourful liveries of their own designs. A seasonal event was the rickshaw races usually won by clever memsahibs who were experts in directing the pullers when to slow down and when to throw in all their physical effort and strength, depending on the terrain.

A popular source of entertainment, and a feature of Simla's social life, was the amateur theatricals conducted by the officers and their wives and sweethearts. Emily Eden describes how in the beginning, female roles were played by men from the artillery and clerks, and sometimes performances had to be postponed owing to quarrels among the cast. It was a matter of pride for a woman to be offered a part in one of the plays presented at the Gaiety, a beautiful little theatre where everybody came in full evening dress, including the viceroy, the C-in-C, and the Punjab governor, all of whom had their special boxes. The theatre was an ideal setting for riotous parties and flirtations and 'hearts were broken and mended again on the stage'.

With its holiday atmosphere, Simla became notorious for its gossip, high living and not-so-harmless flirting. Those who went on leave and after the ladies were called 'poodle fakers' and were said 'to come down the hills fighting rearguard actions against the husbands coming up'. ADCs were another great attraction for the ladies. Gorgeously dressed, an ADC in his evening garb with gold buttons and velvet cuffs appeared to eager young ladies the passport to gaiety and thrills of the viceregal lodge. Even Emily Eden had a soft spot for good-looking ADCs.

It was a closely knit community where everyone knew rather too much about everyone else's affairs. The favourite topic of conversation was about people and parties; who was going out with so and so and who was giving a big party and who were not invited there. Besides, no secret was safe from the army of servants in the sahibs' households. When there was a romantic rendezvous behind Jakko Hill, the rickshaw-pullers feigned to be asleep.

A much talked-about event was the annual Sipi Fair held near Simla where the local girls were displayed to the prospective bridegrooms. The Europeans mingled with the hill folk in their holiday mood. Amateur artists among them used this opportunity to make sketches of hill women in colourful costumes, laden with jewellery.

The Christ Church on the Ridge came to life on Sunday mornings when glamorous memsahibs sporting wide-brimmed straw hats with ostrich feathers arrived there in rickshaws. The viceroy would appear in his carriage to join the crowd for a brief sermon by the archdeacon of Simla. Service was, however, more of a ritual than anything else. The archdeacon was a man of the world and his relations with the ladies of Simla were regarded as 'tender without being romantic and confiding without being burdensome'. The viceregal atmosphere of Simla lent him a special air of authority and he was among the first to hear whispers of scandals, flirtations and engagements.

It was during the 1880s that Kipling immortalized Simla with his *Plain Tales from the Hills* which led many to regard Simla 'as a centre of frivolity, jealousy and intrigue and populated by frivolous grass widows and idle hill captains'. The famous Peleti's Grand Hotel, the popular meeting place of Englishmen and -women, was the centre of romantic escapades as seen from Kipling's lines put in the mouth of the virtuous monkey who boasted:

> Never in my life
> Have I flirted at Peleti's
> With another Bandar's wife.

Kipling caught the spirit of Simla in the following verses:

> 'Mabel', 'Officers', 'goodbye',
> Glamour, wine and witchery—
> On my soul's sincerity,
> 'Love like ours can never die!'
>
> . . .
>
> So long as aces take the kind,
> or backers take the bet,
> So long as debt leads men to wed,
> Or marriage leads to debt
> So long as little luncheons, love
> And scandal hold their vogue,
> Or whisky at Jutogh,
> If you love me as I love you
> What knife can cut our love in two?

Kipling's image of the typical hill station memsahib was that she was 'frivolous, vain, sometimes adulterous, with an ever-twinkling laugh and the occasional soft spot for a handsome subaltern'. His writings with hints of loose living among the elite of Simla irritated the government circles and some of them dismissed him as a 'subversive pamphleteer' given to criticize his betters. Others attributed his stories of life in Simla to 'the natural envy of a cad who had sought and been refused an entree to Simla society'. Nonetheless, there was no getting away from reality and even Lady Dufferin's book *Our Viceregal Life in India* did suggest that pleasure-seeking was the chief occupation of many Simla residents. Writing at the turn of the twentieth century, Maud Diver pleaded for a 'more sympathetic understanding' of the Englishwoman and held Kipling's assertions about the 'lower tone of social morality' to be 'unjust and untrue'. All the same, she did admit that the behaviour of her 'exiled sisters' was not always blameless in the ambience of Simla while away from their husbands. She noted:

> The proverbial relations between Satan and idle hands is too often confirmed in the Himalaya, and for a woman who is young, comely and gifted with a taste for acting, Simla is assuredly not the most innocuous place on God's earth. Here frivolity reaches its highest point and social pleasures are, to all appearance, the end and aim of everyone's existence.

Simla thus became the hot news in media both in India and England. There were feature articles under such headlines as 'Revels in Olympus'. A defence was put forward that newspaper correspondents in Simla had nothing much to report since government business was conducted with such discretion that there was rarely any hard news worth reporting. But as they had to fill up space somehow, they paid undue attention to the gaiety of the place. It was also said that many husbands coming to Simla for investigation of scandals communicated to them by their well-wishers, found nothing more than gossip and returned to their desks with doubts allayed. Whatever the case, this kind of defence was never really accepted. It was concluded that 'wherever youth and beauty meet, there will no doubt be some scandal and gossip'. There was a lot of chit-chat about pretty and indiscreet women. There was said to be a hotel in Simla where a separation bell was rung by the manager early in the morning to warn his guests to return to their own beds. Much in circulation among the soldiers was the reported remark of a Calcutta prostitute that she and her colleagues refrained from going to Simla as they felt they were in no position to compete with amateurs.

All said and done, despite the butterfly reputation of Simla, the British managed to rule one-fifth of mankind from that remote Himalayan resort linked to the outside world by a narrow precipitous road. As the imperial sun reached its zenith, communications with Simla were transformed by the construction of the Kalka–Simla railway (1903), an outstanding feat of imperial engineering. The arrival of the railway brought a sea change in the pattern of Simla's life. It became ever more obvious, more public, more informal. The old small-town days of private parties, concerts, fairs, etc., where everyone knew everyone were finally over.

11

Nautch Parties

The word 'nautch' is an anglicized form of the Hindi/ Urdu word nach derived from the Sanskrit nritya through the Prakrit nachcha, meaning dance. Nautch represented cultural interaction between the natives and early English settlers in India. Its professional exponent, the nautch girl, held the white sahib spellbound for nearly two centuries. 'Delicate in person, soft in her features, perfect in form', she captivated the hearts of ordinary Englishmen by her grace and charm, enthralled the more sophisticated among them by her conversation and wit and enraptured the elite with her nautch which some of them found 'superior to all the operas in the world'.

Professional nautch girls and their performances have been described in numerous journals, travelogues, memoirs and diaries left by European visitors, missionaries, and civil and military officials. The fare provided by nautch girls fascinated most viewers and many a sahib was captivated by their seductive charms. The post-Plassey British nabobs who had made quick fortunes emulated the ostentatious lifestyle of native princes and omrahs. They even maintained their own troupes of nautch girls and musicians for the entertainment of their guests. A dinner in the community was usually followed by a nautch performance. So were other festive occasions, such as the celebration of a King Emperor's birthday and visits of dignitaries to civil and military stations. Nautch girls would also accompany the British army whenever it was on the move, entertaining the soldiers on the way. At times they were also engaged to welcome arriving guests on the highways. An army officer in his journal (1783) states that he was met by his 'friend Major MacNeal who was preceded by a troupe of nautch girls. The latter encircled his palanquin, dancing until he entered the Major's house in Arcot.'

Three nautch girls represent different figures indicative of the different passions described in the song which accompanies the dance (by C. Belnos c. 1820)

So popular was this entertainment, especially with the soldiers that nautch girls began to move en masse to British stations. Captain Williamson notes in his *Costumes and Customs of Modern India* (1813) that between the years 1778 and 1785, many outstanding dancing girls quit the cities and retired to the cantonments, where they were received with open arms. Quite often, lonely men would send for nautch girls to entertain them in their own houses. Usually, groups of civilians or soldiers joined hands to hire nautch girls for an evening of amusement. They would often recite songs learnt from them and even translate them into popular ditties.

Nautch girls catered to a mixed society but it was men who got into the spirit of the nautch. Encouraged by the men's applause of wah, wah they would shed their stiff reserve and cool propriety, displaying their seductive charms. Captain Godfrey Charles Mundy (1832) in his journal mentions, 'when European ladies attend a nautch, the dancing girls are warned beforehand and they only witness a graceful and sufficiently stupid display.'

James Forbes in his *Oriental Memoirs* (1813) pays this compliment to nautch girls:

> They are extremely delicate in their person, soft and regular in their features, with a form of perfect symmetry, and although dedicated from infancy to this profession, they in general preserve a decency and modesty in their demeanour, which is more likely to allure than the shameless effrontery of similar characters in other countries.

The quality of the nautch and the class of nautch girls varied from place to place as did the reactions of the British spectators. In a typical early nineteenth-century account, Captain Mundy describes a splendid nautch party held in honour of the commander-in-chief by the Company's political agent, Captain Wade, in Ludhiana, where forty-six nautch girls entertained the guests, only to be surpassed by the British resident at Delhi who honoured the commander-in-chief with a performance by a hundred nautch girls.

In another account, nautch girls are portrayed as 'pretty gazelle-eyed damsels arrayed in robes of sky-blue, crimson and gold in stately guise whose languishing glances stare brightly through their antimonial borders.'

The nautch became a common form of entertainment in the mansions of the English merchants-turned-rulers in Bengal and other parts of India. In 1791, the governor of Madras entertained the nawab of Carnatic at a dinner with a nautch by girls of the devadasi community. This custom continued till the first half of the nineteenth century. Calcutta, the capital of the Raj, was known to be the stronghold of nautch. Wealthy Bengalis vied with one another in inviting famous nautch girls, even from faraway Lucknow and Delhi, for the entertainment of their European guests. The annual Durga Puja festival celebrated with great pomp was a special occasion for nautch parties. Invitations were issued through letters and cards couched in a florid style as well as through advertisements in the local press. At times, some influential babus succeeded in securing the presence of the Governor General, the commander-in-chief or other high dignitaries at these celebrations. Here is a news report from the *Calcutta Gazette* of 20 October 1814:

Raja Nob Kishen's nautch party at Calcutta. The Raja is entertaining a fashionable party of Europeans to a nautch performance (by Sir Charles D'oyly, c. 1825)

The Hindoo holidays of Durga Puja have begun. Many of the rich Hindoos vying with one another in expenses and profusion endeavour by the richness of their festivals to get a name amongst men. The principal days of entertainment are the 20th, 21st and 22nd; on which Nickee will warble her lovely ditties at the hospitable mansion of Raja Kishun Chand Roy . . . Nor will the hall of Neel Mony Mullick resound less delightfully with the affecting strains of Ushoorun who for compass of voice and variety of note excels all the damsels of Hindostan. Misree whose graceful gestures would not hurt the practised eye of Parisot will lead the fairy dance on the boards of Joy Kishun Roy's happy dwelling . . .

Mrs S.C. Belnos, a reputed artist who lived in Calcutta in the early nineteenth century, invested nautch girls with a romantic aura. In her vivid description of a dance party held in Calcutta during the Puja festival, she observed:

On entering the magnificent saloon, the eye is dazzled by a blaze of lights from splendid lustres, triple wall shades, chandle brass, etc., superb pier glasses, pictures, sofas, chairs, Turkey carpets, etc., adorn the splendid hall; these combined with the sounds of different kinds of music, both European and Indian, played all at the same time in different apartments; the noise of native tom-toms from another part of the house; the hum of human voices, the glittering dresses of the dancing girls, their slow and graceful movement; the rich dresses of the Rajah and his equally opulent Indian guests; the gay circle of European ladies and gentlemen, and the delicious scent of attar of roses and sandal which perfumes the saloon, strikes the stranger with amazement; but he fancies himself transported to some enchanted region, and the whole scene before him is but a fairy vision.

These splendid parties of nautch entertainment were covered by the local press, especially when dignitaries graced them with their presence. We find several absorbing accounts of nautch performances at Delhi, Bombay, Madras and other places. Observing that Delhi was the place where native dancing was to be seen in its perfection, Lieutenant Thomas Bacon (1831) gives a graphic description of a nautch held there in a spacious tent laid out for this purpose by Maharaja Hindu Rao:

> The tent was most glaringly lighted, *mussaulchi*s or torch bearers stood here and there ready to attend to any person who might require them . . . we had scarcely seated ourselves ere two of them made their appearance, floating into our presence, all tinsel coloured muslin and ornaments: they were followed by three musicians, and attended by a couple of *mussaulchi*s who held their torches first to the face and then lower down as if showing off the charms of the dancers to the best advantage.

There is another fascinating description by Lieutenant Colonel Torrens (1860) of a nautch by Kashmiri girls in the picturesque Shalimar Gardens at Srinagar. The author was enchanted by the beauty of Shalimar, the queen of gardens, which he felt should be visited at night by the pale of moonlight when it is properly bedecked with torches, and crowned with lamps. Then 'the proper thing to do is to give orders for a nautch at Shalimar.' Apart from the beauty of the place, Torrens was enchanted with the dancing and singing of the charming Kashmiri nautch girls whom he considered 'vastly superior' to what he had seen elsewhere. Another witness to a similar performance in Shalimar Gardens was a reputed professional artist, William Simpson, who was so enthralled by the sight of nautch girls dancing by torchlight that he describes it as 'the sweet delusion of a never-to-be-forgotten night'.

The immense popularity of the nautch can be judged by the fact that at times a dance performance would begin in the evening and last until daybreak. Among the prominent and most colourful British residents of Delhi at that time were Colonel James Skinner, known as Secunder Sahib, and Sir David Ochterlony, nicknamed Loony Akhtar, who lived in royal style and held lavish nautch parties to entertain the English community. Colonel Skinner, a great patron of Delhi artists, would give away miniature paintings of nautch girls to his guests, sometimes of the very same dancers who were entertaining them.

Most of the descriptions by Europeans about nautch are, however, repetitive but there is a singularly interesting one by Sir Charles D'oyly from his long burlesque poem entitled *Tom Raw the Griffin* (1828):

> See! how invitingly the creatures dance!
> What elegance and ease in every motion!
> Not as the ladies do at home, or France,
> So turbulent and full of strange commotion;
> Of this our Indian fair have an odd notion;
> Their step is slow and measured—not a caper
> That lifts them from the ground,—but grave devotion
> To time, and suppleness of figure's taper,
> It is no doubt the modestest—at least on paper!
>
> Or how describe the graceful play of arms,
> Which, beautifully waving, as they move,
> Reveals, at every step, a thousand charms;
> Expressing terror, languishment, or love;
> While their dark, speaking eye, unceasing rove
> O'er all around—Few know the ditty's meaning:
> And—to speak truth, 'tis ten to twenty you've
> Not learnt the language, though—your dullness screening,
> You shout applause, as if the tongue au fait you'd been in
>
> See the Circassian—'tis a pleasing sight,
> With uplift arms her filmy veil is spread,

Like a transparent canopy, and light
As cobwebs on the lawn on which you tread.
Rolling from side to side her airy head
Swift as the agile roe's elastic bound;
Then, in a giddy evolution led,
Her full robes, whirling, gracefully around,
She sinks amidst her sparkling drap'ry to the ground.

Captain Mundy found the dress of a nautch girl infinitely more decent than that of French and Italian figurines, but as a keen observer he noticed that 'the upper portion of the costume . . . is not quite so impervious to sight as a bodice of more opaque texture than muslin might render it'.

From contemporary accounts one finds that one of the most popular numbers in the repertoire of the nautch girl was the 'Kahar-ka nautch' or 'Kuharwa', the bearer's dance, which was usually performed before a male audience. While rendering it the nautch girl would tie a sash round her loins, through which she pulled up her gown and put another across her shoulders. Twisting a turban saucily round her head she would let her long black hair fall on her back and around her bosom and then dart forward with animated gestures, something of the nature of a highland fling.

Another popular number considered graceful was the kite dance performed to the rhythm of a slow and expressive melody. The dancers would imitate in their gestures the movements of a person flying a kite. Commenting on this dance, one army officer observed that 'the attitudes incident to this performance are most favourable to Indian grace and suppleness and the heavenward direction of the eyes displays these features, as doubtless my fair country women know, to the very best advantage.' Among others, mention may be made of the 'snake dance' where the nautch girl would put the ends of the dupatta in her mouth and mimic playing the gourd for charming a snake.

In south India, the dance tradition continued to be associated with the temple. While kathak flourished in north India, dassi attam, also referred to as sadir nautch, dominated the nautch scene in the south. It was far more than mere visible expression of a sung melody. It had a life of its own with a direct appeal to emotions. Often the dance was in itself the pantomime of a whole story. Dr John Shortt in his account of *Dancing Girls of S. India* (1870) noted that their dance movements were marked by agility, ease and gracefulness, and the turning and twisting of their hands, eyes, face, features and trunk were in complete harmony with their nimble steps whilst they beat time with their feet. Their dance was more feminine and suited to solo performances in temples and later in a court and at other public functions. There was greater emphasis on pure dance and *abhinaya* or expressions as they recited songs which were generally in praise of the gods but could also be interpreted in human terms for the benefit of their patrons.

The songs of nautch girls had as their themes either the amorous escapades in the lives of gods or conventional romantic tales, usually about the lover's yearning for the beloved. Until the end of the nineteenth century, songs in Persian were as popular as those in Hindi. The one Persian ghazal by Hafiz which dominated the nautch scene for over a hundred years and invariably evoked roaring applause both from the natives and from the Europeans was '*Tazah ba Tazah Nu ba Nu*' (Fresh and Fresh, New and New). A mirthful melody in which the poet recommends applying the principles of fresh and new to all he does, whether in drinking, making friends, or making love. This finds mention in numerous foreign accounts of the nautch. There are even references comparing the singing style and the rendering of this ghazal by several nautch girls of the day.

The nautch girls had a repertoire of songs, which became so popular with the sahibs that they got them translated into English verse. The *Calcutta Gazette* of 9 June 1808 carried a contribution from a correspondent who said:

Happening to attend a Cashmerian [sic] nautch a few nights ago, I was struck with the melody and effect of one of the native airs, which so much attracted my attention that I procured a copy and version of the song. The original is in the Cashmeree language, and the version has only the merit of being faithful:

Sleep! Sleep! let me sing thee to sleep,
Sleep while my tresses over thee
Fall in fragrant caress.
Sleep, for to watch thee reposing
Is to me deep happiness.
Sleep, sleep, let me sing thee to sleep.

Wake! wake! let me kiss thee awake.
Wake from thy dreams of beauty
To the warmth of a real embrace.
Wake from the chain of night's shadowy thrall.
Wake! See the morn in my face!
Wake, wake, let me kiss thee awake.

Stay! stay! let me pray thee to stay.
That the red light of returning day!
'Tis but the gleam of his evening ray,
That slants through the lattice still
Stay, stay, let me pray thee to stay!

Until the middle of the nineteenth century, many Company officials were familiar with the Persian language and took interest in Persian poetry. There were even a few who would compose extempore couplets in Persian. These popular songs devoted to wine and women aroused romantic feelings and amorous desires among the audience. The visual display of human emotions served to enhance the appeal of the melodies as the spectators saw in them a reflection of their own hopes and aspirations. When a nautch girl addressed a patron with whom she had a liaison, the song would convey a meaningful message to him.

The nautch was thus an institution about which most sahibs had something to say. Exciting or boring, graceful or awkward, glamorous or dull, the opinions expressed were usually subjective. As Mrs Mildred Archer, an authority on paintings by European artists in India during the Raj, says:

> Judgement depended as much on who you were as on what you saw. Were you solemnly approaching the nautch as a serious part of Indian culture or were you accepting it as a frolicsome amusement which had beguiled countless Indians including the Mughal Emperors Akbar and Jehangir?

As the nineteenth century wore on, the spread of English education brought in a new petit bourgeois class which, influenced by Western ideas, got alienated from the art and cultural traditions of the country. This educated group was also swayed by the writings of some foreign observers who, without understanding the origin and nature of the Indian dance art and mistaking it for a representation of erotic temple sculptures, condemned it as 'repulsive and immoral'. They made no distinction between an accomplished professional nautch girl or a devadasi and a common prostitute, dubbing both as fallen women. The educated Indians, suffering from an inferiority complex, were overcome with a sense of shame about their own traditional arts.

By this time, the missionaries in their efforts to propagate the virtues of the Christian civilization denounced Indian religious practices, social customs, and manners. The nautch institution in particular came under heavy attack as it was taken up as a moral issue. Some missionaries went to the extent of saying that nautch aroused anti-Christian feelings.

In their drive against nautch, the missionaries were also joined by a powerful group of educated Indian social reformers who, influenced by Western ideas and Victorian moral values, had lost pride in their own cultural heritage. In 1892, they started an 'anti-nautch' movement in Madras, which spread to other parts of the country as well. This movement was in a way inspired by the Madras Christian Literature Society which had launched virulent propaganda against nautch girls invited by the local gentry for a performance in honour of British dignitaries.

Among the missionaries, the crusade was led by Reverend J. Murdoch who launched a series of publications on Indian social reform in which his main target were nautch girls, who were condemned in extremely harsh terms. They were accused of impoverishing and ruining their patrons. The British official elite were urged to refrain from attending functions where nautch entertainment was provided. In an exclusive pamphlet addressed to English ladies, they were advised never to attend any such gathering themselves and to use all their influence to prevent their husbands from doing so.

Another publication entitled *Nautches—An Appeal to Educated Hindus* highlighted the evil effects of nautches ranging from loss of money, bodily weakness and disease to injurious influence upon one's character.

The anti-nautch campaign gathered momentum with the support of the Indian press and the Social Purity associations sponsored by the Purity movement in England for reform of public and private morals. One Miss Tennant even came all the way from England to persuade educated Indians to boycott their own dances. The Punjab Purity Association launched a forceful drive against nautches and published a booklet containing the opinions of eminent Punjabis vehemently condemning nautch girls. The booklet highlighted the denunciation of nautch by eminent reformer Keshub Chandra Sen who described a nautch girl as a:

> 'hideous woman . . . Hell is in her eyes. In her breast is a vast ocean of poison. Round her comely waist dwell the furies of hell. Her hands are brandishing unseen daggers ever ready to strike unwary or wilful victims that fall in her way. Her blandishments are India's ruin. Alas! her smile is India's death.

Some agitators, who belonged to the Hindu Social Reform Association of Madras, appealed to the governor of Madras and the viceroy in 1893 to discourage what they said was a 'pernicious' entertainment by declining to attend any function at which nautch girls were invited to perform. They also solicited the support of the Excellencies in their efforts to remove this evil practice on the ground that it had no sanction of religion, nor any claim to be considered a national institution. However, both the viceroy and the governor, who had been present on several occasions on which nautches had been performed and had not found anything 'which might in the remotest degree be considered improper', turned down their plea.

The Indian press, not satisfied with the replies of the viceroy and the governor, continued to plead for official support for the anti-nautch campaign. The *Madras Mail* urged Europeans to back the anti-nautch campaign by pointing out, 'the Hindu social reformer is the product of our western education, and he must not be left to struggle on alone.' However, Viceroy Lansdowne, who privately expressed his dislike for nautches, recorded: 'I am not much inclined to surrender at discretion to these well-meaning but intolerant gentlemen.'

The combined arguments of the reformers and the press failed to persuade the government to take any action in the matter. However, the anti-nautch campaign continued in full blast and the National Social Conference at its meeting in Madras in 1894 adopted a resolution condemning nautches. The Bengali journal *Sanjivani* of 8 December assailed the lieutenant governor of Bengal, Sir Charles Elliot, for attending a nautch. Later, when Lord Curzon was approached by the reformers, he dismissed the issue as of little concern, not deserving any pronouncement or action on his part.

The reformers were, however, greatly encouraged by one Mrs Marcus Fuller, wife of an English missionary in Bombay, who in her book *The Wrongs of Indian Womanhood,* published in 1900, strongly condemned the nautch institution and the practice of dedicating girls to temples. She reminded the reformers to keep knocking at the doors of the Viceregal Lodge till the government took a policy decision against the viewing of nautch.

The persistent efforts of the reformers eventually bore fruit in 1905 when a decision was taken not to provide nautch entertainment at the reception that was held in honour of the Prince of Wales in Madras.

The advent of All-India Radio and cinema provided opportunities for a few talented artists to practise their profession but most of them sank into oblivion. And so, honoured by royal lovers, rewarded by nawabs and nobles, patronized by the European elite, immortalized by poets and chroniclers, and pursued by lovesick gallants, the Indian nautch girl, a symbol of glamour, grace and glory, and queen of performing arts, passed into the pages of history.

12

Palanquin Pleasure

The most common and popular mode of conveyance until 1850 was the palanquin or palkee, a carriage without wheels, for one person, conveyed on the shoulders of men by means of a pole proceeding from each extremity which they supported. Four or more bearers carried the palanquin and the occupant reclined at full length on an elastic mattress with back and side cushions to match. The bottom in some cases was caned like a chair and cushions covered with morocco leather.

The palanquins available for hire in the towns were called ticca palkees. According to a report of 1840, the charges for a day's hire in Calcutta were one rupee four annas, of which the bearers paid four annas for the use of the palanquin which was hired by them from a stand of palanquins belonging to another individual. At the same time, short trips with payments according to time or distance yielded higher earnings to the bearers. Most sahibs, however, chose to have their own private palanquins and maintained their own set of bearers on monthly wages of four to five rupees. Private bearers usually carried their master to his office in the morning and home in the evening but were at his and the family's service all day. Whenever the master went to a distant place, above the ordinary distance, two more men would be engaged.

Newly-weds going on a honeymoon (by G.F. Atkinson, c. 1859)

There is an interesting account of a general strike by the palanquin bearers in Calcutta in 1828. The palanquin bearers were all natives of Orissa and opposed the regulation requiring mandatory registration of palanquins and wearing of brass badges by the bearers. There was great opposition to the badges as the bearers claimed that this would involve the loss of their caste. The authorities, however, remained adamant and, negotiations proving fruitless, the Oriya bearers assembled in a body at the Chowringhee maidan. They refused to work and talked of marching en masse back to Orissa. In the meantime, other commonly termed Hindostanee, up-country or

Rouwanee bearers, made their appearance in Calcutta. This struck a blow to the monopoly of the Oriya bearers who, realizing their situation, came to terms with the authorities. Palanquins were numbered, rates fixed and the bearers ticketed.

The carrying of a palanquin required the bearers to take great care in regulating their paces, in order to avoid jolting or tossing the occupant who in turn had to maintain the balance of the carriage by keeping himself as much as possible in the centre of the seat. Whenever the balance was disturbed, the bearers would remonstrate and bestir the traveller from his delightful reverie or snooze. The sahib's peon or messenger usually walked along by the side of the door and at night, torch-bearers or mashalchis led the way. The cavalcade of a person of rank included chubdars, with large silver walking-staffs, marching in front. The native chiefs and princes, when travelling in their ornamented and gilded palanquins, were preceded by drummers and flutists and announcers of the titles and supernatural alliances of these high and mighty.

Long-distance travel from one town to another was also undertaken in palanquins. The East India Company organized the system of *dawk palkee* which provided for day-and-night travel with fresh sets of bearers being posted at certain fixed points on the road. The average speed came to about four to five miles an hour. Four bearers at a time carried the palanquin, and they were relieved by an equal number by rotation after a run of eight or ten minutes, during which time they also shifted the burden from one shoulder to the other. People preferred to travel in the coolness of the night and they were protected from the approach of wild beasts by the blaze of torches carried by men of this calling.

Albert Hervey in his account (1850) of travel to Vellore by palanquin wrote: 'These poor fellows run for upwards of thirty miles, with scarcely any rest, at the rate of four miles an hour, taking little or no sustenance all the time. When they arrive at the end of their stage, they put down their load and walk off.' It was possible to cover a distance of up to a hundred miles a day. The dawk palkee was fitted with such conveniences as extra drawers and pockets, lamps, hat slings, glass and bottle racks, and firearm receptacles.

Before commencing travel by dawk palkee, it was necessary to approach the head of the postal department informing him about one's destination and the duration of stay at the halting stations. Dawk bungalows or rest houses were located at every twenty miles on the road from Delhi to Calcutta, at which the traveller found accommodation and attendance. A plain dish of fowl curry and rice, or perhaps a leg of mutton and potatoes, would be provided for meals. The traveler was obliged to carry other items such as tea, sugar, wine and bread. However, European residents in the neighbourhood offered generous hospitality to their fellow countrymen travelling in their area even when there were no letters of introduction and they were perfect strangers. One writer in 1843 noted, 'everywhere you find the most hearty welcome, and the most hospitable reception. The longer the guest is pleased to remain, the greater is the satisfaction which he gives to the host.'

We have an interesting account by a traveller who went from Delhi to Agra by a dawk palkee in the 1840s, a distance of 137 miles for which he paid 140 rupees.

I engaged eight bearers to carry my palanquin. Besides these I had four *bangy burdars,* men who are each obliged to carry forty pound weight, in small wooden or tin boxes, called *petarrah*s, resting on the shoulder, and two *masalchi*s or torch-bearers. From Delhi to Agra there are twelve stages, the longest fourteen, the shortest ten miles. An express acquaints the postmasters beforehand of the approach of travellers, so that the new bearers are always found ready. When we approached a new stage all the bearers set up a shrill cry to announce that they were coming. The torch-bearer runs by the side of the palanquin occasionally feeding his cotton torch with oil, which he carries with him in a wooden bottle, or a bamboo.

At every change of bearers, the relieved men invariably petition for *bukshish,* and if they do not receive something the new men annoy the traveller by jolting him or doing their duty lazily. It may be easily conceived that travelling in this mode is not the most pleasant, however luxurious it may appear to be.

One woman on the other hand wrote cheerfully in 1838: 'I can sleep a good part of the night and being able to sit up or lie down at pleasure, with plenty of room, I find it far less fatiguing than being cramped up all day on a carriage.'

T. Rev. Acland, an English clergyman in the 1840s, enjoyed the chanting of his palanquin-bearers as they marched forward on dusty roads. He wrote:

They keep to the same sing-song time, yet they generally invent the words as they go along . . . Each line is sung in a different voice. In the following, for instance, the first line would be sung in the usual voice, the second very high, the third on a sort of gruff tone:

Oh, what heavy bag!
No; it's an elephant:
He is an awful weight.

Let's throw his palkee down—
Let's set him in the mud—
Let's leave him to his fate.
No, for he'll be angry then;
Ay, and he will beat us then
With a thick stick.
Then let's make haste and get along,
Jump along quick.

And then, suiting the action to the word, off they set in a nasty jog-trot which rattled every bone in my body, keeping chorus all the time of 'jump along quick, jump along quick', until they were obliged to stop for laughing. The second sample is from the men who carried Mrs Acland, and is in quite a different metre.

She's not heavy,
Cubbadar! Little baba,
Cubbadar! Carry her swiftly,
Cubbadar! Pretty baba
Cubbadar! Cubbadar!
Cubbadar!

Trim the torches,
Cubbadar! For the road's rough
Cubbadar! Here the bridge is,
Cubbadar! Pass it swiftly,
Cubbadar! Cubbadar!
Cubbadar!

Carry her gently,
Cubbadar! Little baba,
Cubbadar! Sing so cheerily,

Cubbadar! Pretty baba,
Cubbadar! Cubbadar!
Cubbadar!

Cubbadar' means 'take care', and 'baba' (pronounced 'barba') means 'young lady.

13

Imperial Pageantry—the Great Delhi Durbars

The nineteenth century is called the British century as it witnessed the emergence of the vast British Empire and its international supremacy in the political and economic affairs of nations. The Empire was glorified with an ideology defined by the high Victorian concept of fair play and justice. This had an appeal for the British people, who would not support an institution that was unfair and contrary to their national code. They were inspired by the sublime importance of the imperial idea as they were convinced it was benign and benevolent. The global imperial structure was bound together by the British Crown.

THE FIRST IMPERIAL DURBAR IN DELHI, 1877

In 1876, Queen Victoria was proclaimed Kaiser-i-Hind, the Empress of India. Lord Lytton, the viceroy, decided to use this occasion to hold a grand Imperial Durbar on an unprecedented scale. It was in keeping with the Indian tradition of the durbar, dazzling celebrations on the occasion of the coronation of a new ruler to mark his sovereignty over his subjects. The durbar was adopted by the East India Company in the late eighteenth century to display its power to native rulers and the people.

By 1800, holding durbars had become a regular practice for the Governor General at Calcutta, where maharajas and nawabs were ceremoniously received. The British emulated the Mughal style and adopted the trappings of Indian royalty with the exercise of power and authority associated with opulence. The public display of imperial grandeur through durbars became a ritual of the Raj.

Although it was only in 1911 that the government decided to transfer the capital from Calcutta to Delhi, the historical importance of Delhi was keenly felt after the Mutiny and the removal of the Mughal emperor to Burma. Lord Lytton decided to hold the spectacular durbar in Delhi to proclaim Queen Victoria as Kaiser-i-Hind. As a representative of the queen, the viceroy bestowed royal honours from time to time. After much planning, Lytton selected a site just outside the Mughal capital of Delhi for his memorable extravaganza scheduled for New Year's Day, 1877.

The viceroy was determined to revive Mughal traditions so as to display the majesty, power and prestige of the Raj. During the closing weeks of 1876, more than four hundred Indian princes and their retinues assembled in Delhi. While the preparations were in full progress, the viceroy arrived on 23 December by train from Calcutta and was received at the station by government officials and many native princes to whom he said on alighting:

Princes, chiefs and nobles—It is with feelings of unusual pleasure I find you here assembled from all parts of India to take part in a ceremonial which I trust will be the means of drawing still closer the bonds of union between the Government of Her Majesty and the great allies and feudatories of the Empire. I thank you for the cordiality with which you have responded to my invitation, and trust the close of our proceedings will confirm the auspicious character of their commencement. Accept my hearty welcome to Delhi!

Scene from The Imperial Durbar 1877

The viceroy and his family seated on elephants were then taken in procession through the city to the royal tent which he entered amid the blare of trumpets and the thunder of royal salutes from many batteries waking the thousand echoes of the walls and forts of Delhi.

During the whole week prior to the great durbar, Lord Lytton received visits from the maharajas, the consuls general, and consuls of foreign European powers, together with a large number of minor chiefs and rajas. The following report on the great Delhi Durbar was carried by the *Illustrated London News* of 6 January 1877:

> Each Prince or chief got a commemorative medal—gold for greater princes, silver for those of inferior rank. The Viceroy himself hung it round each chief's neck, while the Foreign Secretary made a short speech in Hindustani to the effect that this was a personal gift from Her Majesty in honour of her assumption of the Imperial title. The medal, which is large and handsome, bears on one side the Queen's head, and on the other words 'Kaiser-i-Hind' in Arabic and Sanscrit characters. Each of the greater chiefs also received a heavy and beautifully worked banner, emblazoned with the arms of his House, and carried on a gilt pole, which bore the inscription, 'From Victoria, Empress of India. 1st January, 1877.' Two stalwart highlanders supported the banner before the throne: and the Viceroy, rising and grasping the pole, addressed to his visitor some such words as these—'let it remind you of the relations between your Princely House and the Paramount Power.

The culminating scene of the Grand Durbar on 1 January 1877 was one of great splendour. The governors, the lieutenant governors, state officials, and sixty-three ruling chiefs attended by their suits and standard-bearers, with magnificent memorial banners, were grouped in a semicircle in front of the throne. Behind them the vast amphitheatre was filled with foreign embassies, and the native nobility and gentry who had received invitations; and further in the rear was the vast concourse of spectators who had assembled to witness the ceremony. The whole scene presented a spectacle of unprecedented brilliance. To the south of the dais fifteen thousand troops were drawn up under arms, including contingents from the Madras and Bombay armies, and the Punjab frontier force. To the north were ranged the minor chiefs, with their troops and retinues. The viceroy arrived at the camp at about half-past twelve, and at once ascended the throne. His Excellency's arrival was heralded by flourishes of trumpets and a fanfare from the massed bands of the various regiments present. A grand march was played, followed by the national anthem.

Major Barnes, the chief herald, then read the proclamation. This part of the ceremony was preceded and followed by flourishes of trumpets, and the imperial standard was then hoisted. The Proclamation was followed by a salute of one hundred and one salvos of artillery of six guns each, and a feu de joie from the troops, the bands playing the national anthem.

The viceroy then addressed the assemblage. He referred to the promises contained in the Queen's Proclamation of November 1858, and fully confirmed them. The princes and the people had found full security under Her Majesty's rule. The viceroy proceeded to explain the reasons for the assumption of the title of Empress, which was intended to be, to the princes and people of India, a symbol of the union of their interests and claim upon their loyal allegiance, with the imperial power giving them a guarantee of impartial protection. The viceroy then severally addressed the civil and military services, and the officers and soldiers of the army and volunteers, conveying to them Her Majesty's cordial sentiments of esteem and honour. He announced also that Her Majesty, with the object of noting public services and private worth, had sanctioned an increase in the number of members of the Order of the Star of India in British India, and had instituted a new order entitled the Order of the Indian Empire.

Addressing the princes and chiefs, the viceroy bid them welcome, and said he regarded their presence as evidence of their attachment to the imperial rule. His Excellency, proceeding to address the natives generally, recognized their claim to participate largely in the administration of the country, and counselled the adoption of the only system of education that would enable them to comprehend and practise the principles of the Queen's government. Referring to the possibility of an invasion, the viceroy said that no enemy could attack the Empire in India without assailing the whole Empire, and pointed out that the fidelity of Her Majesty's allies provided ample power to repel and punish assailants. The viceroy concluded by reading the following telegraphic message from the Queen:

> We, Victoria, by the grace of God, of the United Kingdom, Queen, Empress of India, send through our Viceroy to all our officers, civil and military, and to all Princes, chiefs, and people now at Delhi assembled, our Royal and Imperial greeting, and assure them of the deep interest and earnest affection with which we regard the people of our Indian Empire. We have witnessed with heartfelt satisfaction the reception which they have accorded to our beloved son, and have been touched by the evidence of their loyalty and attachment to our house and throne. We trust that the present occasion may tend to unite in bonds of yet closer affection ourselves and our subjects, that, from the highest to the humblest, all may feel that, under our rule, the great principles of liberty, equity, and justice are secured to them, and that to promote their happiness, to add to their prosperity, and advance their welfare, are the ever-present aims and objects of our Empire.

The address was received with general and prolonged cheering, and after three cheers from the troops, the viceroy declared the assemblage dissolved. The ceremony of the proclamation was performed with all pomp of heraldry by the chief herald, Major Barnes, and his assistants. The whole assemblage was encircled by an unbroken line of elephants with gorgeous trappings, and the vast masses of spectators. The weather was splendid. Most of the camps, in addition to their other decorations, displayed the Danish colours, in honour of the Princess of Wales.

After the great ceremony in Delhi on Monday, Maharaja Scindia and the native chiefs sent a telegraphic message to the Queen congratulating her on the assumption of the title of Empress of India. It is stated that on the occasion of the proclamation of the new title fifteen thousand nine hundred and eighty-eight good-conduct prisoners were liberated. The viceroy gave a state banquet in the evening to the governors, lieutenant governors, and high officials. At the reception in the drawing room tent many chiefs were present, glittering with clothes of gold and jewels. The uniforms of every kind, the dresses of the ladies, the pearls and diamonds of the princess made up a wonderful blaze of colour and flash.

One of the brightest features of the celebration was a release of prisoners, again in keeping with an established Indian tradition of royal festivities. Including convicts in the Andaman Isles, about sixteen thousand prisoners were set free. The poor were not forgotten either, for the new Empress rupee was lavishly distributed among them in Delhi. At night Delhi was brilliantly illuminated and large crowds of people assembled on the plain between the Fort and the Jama Masjid to witness the fireworks, which in splendour were said to surpass anything of the kind ever seen before in India.

On the whole, the first imperial durbar at Delhi was well organized in a very dignified and impressive fashion. It succeeded in binding the Indian princes who ruled one-third of India more closely to the British Crown, the ceremonial centre of the British Empire.

LORD CURZON'S DURBAR, 1903

A quarter of a century later, the celebration of Edward VII's coronation, offered a befitting occasion to the viceroy, Lord Curzon, to hold a second great durbar at Delhi in 1903. The choice of Delhi was dictated both for its historic importance, with its striking association with India's past, and for its being more accessible to people travelling from all over the country. Curzon took great pride in the mighty British Empire and to him the durbar was the outward and visible sign of a contented and peaceful India united under British rule. Considered

Scene from the Imperial Durbar 1903

an instrument for the good of humanity, he supported the economic development of India and is remembered for his conservation of ancient Indian monuments, including the Taj Mahal and the Khajuraho temples.

Easily the most memorable and spectacular event of his time in India was the Great Durbar, more famous as Lord Curzon's Durbar, which far surpassed Lytton's in splendour and magnificence—great pageantry, as was never seen before. Curzon personally planned it, occupying centre stage from beginning to end. The durbar area was so large that a five-mile railway line was built to transport visitors to different parts.

The focal point of the durbar was the central amphitheatre. The crowning event of the ceremonies was the dazzling procession on New Year's Day when the viceroy and his lady, seated on a resplendent elephant and preceded by a dazzling procession of mounted police, camels and horses adorned with gold cloth with hanging ornaments, made their state entry, to the tinkling music of anklets, to the durbar arena. The procession marching through the streets of Delhi was watched by over a million people. The durbar was an enchanting scene of splendour with Indian princes sparkling with jewels and a galaxy of ambassadors from all over the world with their colourful costumes adding glamour to the occasion.

The events started on 29 December 1902 and continued for ten days of the New Year. There were sports tournaments, a review of troops, and an investiture ceremony at the Diwan-e-Aam of Red Fort when awards and titles were bestowed on Britons and Indians for their loyalty. A novel feature of the celebrations was an exhibition of Indian arts and crafts—carpets, silks, carvings, paintings, jewellery and antiquities—whose sale was arranged through Thomas Cook. The programme had been planned in advance down to the minutest detail—a special Police Act was enforced to prevent any infringements, including soliciting for prostitutes.

The durbar show was concluded with a full imperial salute of 101 guns before Curzon gave his speech in a manner similar to the one made by the British monarch at the opening session of the Parliament. He concluded saying that for future prosperity, peace and harmony, it was imperative to have unchallenged supremacy of the paramount power under the authority of the British Crown.

THE CORONATION DURBAR, 1911

The third and the last durbar to be held in Delhi was the great Coronation Durbar of 1911 when, at his own insistence, King Emperor George V and Queen Mary appeared in person for the glittering ceremony. The King Emperor wore on this occasion a specially made imperial crown studded with diamonds worth £60,000. This show in its grandeur and spectacle far surpassed Lord Curzon's extravaganza of 1903. The Durbar of 1877 was held on 1 January and this date was since set apart for the annual celebration of the Proclamation of the Empire, and it was on this day that Edward's Coronation Durbar had been held in 1903. The same date in 1911 clashed with Mohurram and it was out of consideration for the Indian Muslim subjects that the King Emperor fixed an earlier day 12 December.

The King and Queen duly arrived at Bombay in December 1911 where their landing was commemorated by the Gateway of India. They arrived in Delhi on 7 December and were taken in a royal procession through the streets of Delhi before reaching the entirely new 'city' of tents set up for the occasion. As many as 233 camps were spread over an area of twenty-five square miles with ten miles of canvas and the construction of sixty miles of new roads and over thirty miles of railway with twenty-four new stations. Two vast concentric amphitheatres were built for the durbar itself; the larger one to hold 100,000 spectators, the smaller one for princes and other notables. The cost of this splendid durbar came to £6,60,000 as against £1,80,000 which Curzon had spent on his tamasha.

The thrones of the King Emperor and Queen Empress occupied the centre on a marble platform under a golden dome. It was here that Their Majesties sat in their royal robes and King George was crowned in person and then received the homage of the princes who provided pomp and colour to the durbar with their customary bejewelled ornamental presence and their equally striking retinue. The King recalled with rare effusiveness, 'the most beautiful and wonderful sight I ever saw'. The most historic and noteworthy event of this spectacle of the Empire was the formal announcement by the King Emperor himself of the transfer of the capital from Calcutta to Delhi.

Their Majesties, the King Emperor and the Queen Empress receiving homage at the Delhi Durbar 1911

The people of Delhi were jubilant that their city had regained its eminent and rightful place as the capital of India. The Bengalis and the British business community had a mixed reception to this news. Before their departure on 15 December, Their Majesties drove from the imperial camp to that of the Government of India nearby and laid there two simple stones to inaugurate the reconstituted capital. His Imperial Majesty expressed supreme satisfaction that 'it has been possible for us before leaving Delhi to lay the first stones of the Imperial capital which will arise from where we now stand.'

The official records acclaimed the success of the durbar as follows:

> The Durbar was the supreme pageant that had brought every one to Delhi, and this unrehearsed spontaneous act of loyalty and homage was certainly the crowning feature of the day. It showed to all the world and the King Emperor himself that his confidence and favour had met with true response; it unveiled the heart of India and showed the real foundation of the Empire. The formalities themselves had been imposingly magnificent and solemnly impressive. As a ceremony, the Durbar was more than a success, it was a triumphant vindication of the wise prescience that planned it: it was carried through with that precision of skilled organization and well-ordered discipline that is characteristic of all British state formalities, and yet it lacked nothing in oriental latitude and that picturesque wealth of pomp and circumstance which the East alone can give. Above all, it brought the King Emperor nearer to the hearts of the Princes and peoples of India, and enabled them to show before the world their deep loyalty and devotion towards the British throne.

14

Exhibition of Animal Fights

Animal fights in India go back to the days of the Mauryan Empire, and later became a favourite pastime of Mughal kings. Akbar was a great patron of fights of wild beasts and for this amusement he got erected a lofty minar just outside the walls of Fatehpur Sikri. Beyond the minar a large space was enclosed from the surrounded plain which served as an arena for the fighting animals. Surrounded by his nobles and omrahs, Akbar would watch from the top of this minar encounters of wild animals, especially elephants, snared for this purpose from neighbouring forests. A large number of animals were kept and trained to fight. They were fed with stimulants to turn them more ferocious and violent in the combat. Akbar look great delight in these amusements but he also encouraged the exhibition of such beastly encounters to rouse the warrior spirit in his men.

Francois Bernier, the French doctor who travelled extensively in Mughal India, describes the elephant fights he witnessed in the sandy bed of the Yamuna River below the Agra Fort:

A wall of earth is raised three or four feet wide and five or six high. The two ponderous beasts meet one another face to face, on opposite sides of the wall. The riders animate the elephant either by soothing words, or by chiding them as cowards, and urge them on with their heels, until the poor creatures approach the wall and are brought to the attack. There are frequent pauses during the fight; it is suspended and renewed; and the mud wall being at length thrown down, the stronger or more courageous elephant passes on and attacks his opponent, and putting him to flight, pursues and fastens upon him with so much obstinacy that the animals can be separated only by means of *cherkys* or fireworks which are made to explode between them.

Capt T. Williamson of the Bengal Army in his classic *Oriental Field Sports* (1819) presents an exhaustive account of Indian hunting traditions and the behaviour patterns of wild animals from boars and buffaloes, to lions, tigers and elephants. He noted that Indian nawabs and princes look special delight in organizing spectacular animal fights on festive occasions. He describes the

A fight between a buffalo and tiger (by S. Howitt, c. 1820)

structure of special enclosures, with full security of the spectators seated in a gallery high enough to command a full view of the area. In a graphic account of a battle between a buffalo and a tiger Williamson recorded:

> The buffalo usually comes out to fight with utmost confidence, conscious of his own prowess. With rapid and furious motions he would charge at the tiger giving it no respite and carry out a war of extermination. According to common belief the buffalo would never quit until a tiger's death proclaimed his victory. In very rare instances the tiger ever came out triumphant.

From later accounts, we find that native princes and nawabs organized special shows of animal fights to entertain English guests. Capt. Mundy describes a series of animal fights arranged by the king of Oudh (1827) in honour of the C-in-C, Lord Combermere, at Lucknow.

> In the centre was erected a gigantic cage of strong bamboos, about fifty feet high, and of like diameter, and roofed with rope network. Sundry small cells, communicating by sliding doors with the main theatre, were tenanted by every species of the savagest inhabitants of the forest. In the large cage, crowded together, and presenting a formidable front of broad, shaggy foreheads well armed with horns, stood a group of buffaloes sternly awaiting the conflict, with their rear against the bamboos. The trapdoors being lifted, two tigers and the same number of bears and leopards, rushed into the cage. The buffaloes instantly commenced hostilities, and made complete shuttlecocks of the bears, who, however, finally escaped by climbing up the bamboos beyond the reach of their horned antagonists. The tigers, one of which was a beautiful animal, fared scarcely better: indeed, the odds were much against them, there being five buffaloes. They appeared, however, to be no match for these powerful creatures, even single-handed, and showed little disposition to be

the assaulters. The larger tiger was much gored in the head, and in return took a mouthful of his enemy's dewlap, but was finally as the fancy would describe it 'bored to the ropes and floored'. The leopards seemed throughout the conflict sedulously to avoid a breach of the peace.

A rhinoceros was next let loose in the open courtyard and the attendants attempted to induce him to pick a quarrel with a tiger who was chained to a ring. The rhinoceros appeared, however, to consider a fettered foe as quite beneath his enmity and having once approached the tiger, and quietly surveyed him, as he writhed and growled, expecting the attack, turned suddenly round and trotted awkwardly off to the yard gate, where he capsized a palanquin which was carrying away a lady fatigued with the sight of these unfeminine sports.

A buffalo and a tiger were the next combatants: they attacked furiously, the tiger springing at the first onset on the other's head, and tearing his neck severely; but he was quickly dismounted, and thrown with such violence as nearly to break his back, and quite to disable him from renewing the combat.

A small elephant was next impelled to attack a leopard. The battle was short and decisive; the former falling on his knee and thrusting his blunted tusks nearly through his antagonist.

Elephant fights were announced as the concluding scene of this day of strife. The spectators took their seats in a long veranda. The narrow stream of the river Gomti runs close under the palace walls, and on the opposite bank a large, open, sandy space presented a convenient theatre for the operations of these gigantic athletes. The elephants educated for the arena were large, powerful males, wrought up to a state of fury by constant feeding with exciting spices. On the spacious plain before us we counted several of these animals parading singly and sulkily to and fro, their mahouts seated on their backs, which were covered with a strong network for the driver to cling by in the conflict. In attendance upon every elephant were two or three men, armed with long spears,

We soon discovered two of the combatants slowly advancing towards each other from opposite sides of the plain. As they approached, their speed gradually increased, and they at length met with a grand shock, entwining their trunks, and pushing, until one, finding himself overmatched, fairly turned tail, and received his adversary's charge in the rear. This was so violent, that the mahout of the flying elephant was dislodged from his seat; he fortunately fell wide of the pursuer, and escaped with a few bruises.

A dead tiger (by Samuel Howitt, c. 1810)

Tigers were often pitted against leopards but the leopards were so powerful that tigers could hardly ever beat them. Even camels were made to fight each other when excited. Common people enjoyed watching fights between rams, who were trained for combat by the butchers and some lower classes.

When Lord William Bentinck, the Governor General, visited Lucknow in 1831, several animal fights were organized for his entertainment. Fanny Parks described some of them:

> Two male elephants were brought in the arena and a female one placed midway. This inflamed the males who attacked each other with their long tusks. They seized each other with their long trunks and interlocked them. When the fight grew fierce, fireworks were thrown to separate them.

She adds that the king had also arranged a fight between two tigers and a horse that had the distinction of killing two tigers earlier. She also saw a combat between rams that attacked each other fiercely fighting with their heads.

John Herbert Caunter, author of the *Oriental Annual* (1853) who witnessed several animal combats, writes about an elephant which fought with three buffaloes and after a long struggle crushed them to death. He also describes fights between two alligators, a leopard and an alligator, a rhinoceros and a buffalo and three wild dogs and a bear. He considered such fights cruel exhibitions which caused more distress than enjoyment to spectators. Not many European guests, however, shared his opinion. Nor did native rulers, who considered animal fights a spectacle.

Bird fights were common. *Murghabazi*, or cockfights, were a popular pastime of the royalty, nobility and commoners alike. Lucknow was the centre of this sport. Even some Europeans living in Lucknow became its devotees and participated in cockfights with the princes and nobles. General Martin was an expert at cockfighting and Nawab Sadat Ali Khan would bet his cocks against those of the general. Col. John Mordaunt, commander of Nawab Asif-ud-daula's bodyguard and a leader of the court revels, was a specialist in the sport and he regularly organized cockfights for the nawab which were attended by the local European gentry. Lord Hastings is reported to have attended Mordaunt's cockfight in April 1784. The cocks were trained and set to fight with spurs and feet as well as their beaks that were specially sharpened by their trainers. When the two cocks were released in the cockpit, their masters stood behind inciting them with, 'my beauty!' and 'go in again'. On hearing these words, the cocks attacked each other with greater fury as if they understood the language of their owners. The fight ended when one of the two got blinded or disabled.

15

Shikar and Pig-sticking

The English sahibs were introduced to big-game hunting by the Indian rulers and princes for whom it had been a traditional outdoor sport from time immemorial. Over the years, as East India Company acquired power and prestige, shikar emerged as the most popular and adventurous sport with civilians and soldiers alike. By the beginning of the nineteenth century, it dominated their outdoor life—no other subject occupies a more prominent place in the Raj literature than shikar. There are countless accounts of hunting expeditions with stories of adventurous encounters with wild animals, including tigers, leopards, lions, hogs and wild buffaloes.

The manly ideal of the nineteenth century, with its stress on physical prowess, expected an Englishman to be a good shot and a good rider. The Raj accepted this manly ideal as the right way for an Englishman to conduct himself both at work and play.

English sportsmen in their lively accounts seem to take the readers with them on their hunting trips and introduce them to the sights, sounds and hazards of the sport. They bring alive the world of animals in the vast jungles of India, from Mysore to the Himalayas. Amongst many books on the subject, perhaps the most comprehensive and informative is *Forty Years among the Wild Animals of India* (1910) by E.C. Hicks of the Imperial Forest Service. The incidents narrated are the pick of his experiences of a long period spent almost entirely in pursuit of big game in dense jungles. His book is a scientific study and a guide for sportsmen. He evolved an assiduous and systematic approach to hunting in order to outwit the most cunning of all animals, namely an experienced old tiger. He observes, 'I have a vague idea of trying on occasions to count up and accounting for over 200 tigers which I have shot, but whether those were all of them, or only half, I could not say in the least.' Laced with anecdotes about the behaviour of animals, he gives details about locations and actual encounters with ferocious wild animals.

Hunting remained one of the most favourite pastimes and the principal diversion of the Englishmen throughout the Raj. It was also considered an essential exercise to enhance the imperial image. Pig-sticking and tiger shooting were the two sports full of excitement and danger. Tiger hunts were grand affairs with dozens of elephants and a big base camp.

The game of games, easily the most popular with civilians and soldiers alike, was pig-sticking, or hog-hunting according to Bombay phraseology. It was in the beginning of the nineteenth century that pig-sticking was recognized as a substitute for bear-sticking, which had till then been the most popular sport of Bengal. The classic centres of this sport were Bengal and the North-West Provinces (UP), and to a lesser extent, Bombay. Madras offered bison and buffalo, while in Assam there was the rhinoceros, but none of these beasts called for those qualities required for the pursuit of the boar.

Pig-sticking was considered an ideal masculine activity requiring strength, toughness and quick wit. From the Governor General to the district officer, it was considered the most exciting and adventurous of field sports. It is recorded that M. Elphinstone, governor of Bombay, would take his whole staff hog-hunting. Daniel Johnson in his *Sketches of Indian Field Sports* (1827) gives a detailed description of the methods of hunting wild boars, instructions for the use of spears, best horses for pig-sticking and how to manage them when hunting. He also points out the dangers and difficulty involved in the game and explains the techniques of surmounting all kinds of problems as well as necessary precautions for the hunters in different seasons of the year. The account is supplemented with a great many anecdotes of hogs and hog-hunters.

Another absorbing account about pig-sticking is contained in Capt. Williamson's classic *Oriental Field Sports* (1819). He gives a vivid description of hog-hunting expeditions and the courage and ferocity of the boars. Besides anecdotes, he advises the hunters on 'how to succeed as a pig-sticker'. Capt. R.S.S. Baden-Powell was an authority on the subject. In his book *Pig-sticking* (1889), a complete guide for pig-stickers, he compares the game to a battlefield as both 'demand the dash and keenness, the pluck and determination for ultimate victory'. Another contemporary writer proclaimed hog-hunting as 'the most entertaining, noble and manly of all sports; the best school for young cavalry officers. They learn to ride better from one day's keen hog-hunting than from a year's exercise with their regiment.' To quote another supporter of pig-sticking, 'the training that makes a sportsman makes a soldier; it gives him endurance and it gives him an eye for a country and familiarity with danger'.

> He on his good steed erect appears
> As when he met the bear,
> But now a worthier foe inspires
> A deadlier game his skill requires.

The civilian officers were also encouraged to take to pig-sticking as in a district they had heavy responsibilities and much loneliness. Pig-sticking helped them preserve their sanity and sense of proportion.

Philip Woodruff, author of *The Men Who Ruled India* (1953), a votary of the sport, observed that anyone engaged in pig-sticking had to be an excellent horseman and 'have a power of quick and cool judgement and a determination not to be beaten'. These qualities were also needed for a good administrator. He added:

> The danger and excitement, the ferocity thus harmlessly given an outlet, sweetened men who might otherwise have been soured by files and hot weather and disappointment, as lime sweetens grass soured by poultry. Ugly lusts for power and revenge melted away and even the lust for women assumed reasonable proportions after a day in pursuit of a pig.

Edward Bradden, another champion propagandist of pig-sticking, offers a graphic account of this exciting sport and practical guidelines for the novice to avoid accidents, in his famous book, *Thirty Years of Shikar* (1895).

> I have seen some accidents from mismanagement of the spear. I have seen a man heavily thrown as a consequence of his running his spear into the ground; I have seen a rider spear his own horse and that of his companion; and any one of these accidents may occur to the novice or to him who is inexpert or careless.

He adds that a boar in its prime is no mean foe 'quick and intrepid in attack, each charge it makes home to its object may leave a wound in horse or rider, and it is like an Englishman in that it does not know when it is beaten.'

Another fascinating account of pig-sticking comes from a sportswoman, Isabel Savory, who was thrilled by this hair-raising sport. 'Pig-sticking is always wildly exciting', she writes (1900).

> No one realises who is near, or what may be in front; it is a case of riding as never before one has ridden; and the excitement of a breakneck gallop only gives place at the finish to a battle royal, fraught with danger. Of more than one gallop after and tussle with a gallant pig it might be written:

> How mad and bad and sad it was!
> And yet, alas! how sweet.

She adds,

> . . . everything was forgotten but the maddening all-engrossing present; the wind in the horses' faces; the rattle of their hoofs and eyes only for one grey object fast disappearing—

> Over the valley, over the level,
> Through the thick jungle, ride like the devil
> Hark forward! a boar! away we go!
> Sit down and ride straight!—tally ho!
> He is a true-bred one—none of your jinking;
> Straight across country—no time for thinking.
> There is water in front!—There's a boar as well;
> Harden your heart; and, ride pell-mell.

16

Beating the Heat

The tropical heat of Indian summers scared the English. Before the introduction of punkhas and American ice in early nineteenth century, they dreaded the oppressive heat and miseries of the hot season. One of the earliest comments on the Indian summer was recorded by an English surgeon in 1774. He refers to his horrible experience on a sultry day 'when not a breath of air was there for many hours; man and every fowl of the air so sensibly felt it, that some species fell down dead'. The heat, dust and hot winds with the awful devastation caused by them earned them the title of angels of death by many a memsahibs in their letters home. It was even jokingly remarked that the deadly heat of Calcutta was more dangerous to British life than any uprising by the natives.

An amusing means to battle the heat in the beastly summer of Calcutta as recommended to sahibs by the English editor of the *Calcutta Gazette* in 1783 was to sleep with Indian women. In fact, the Portuguese actually secured a firman from Emperor Shahjahan to keep Bengali women during summer to save them from the heat of the delta. A verse from Lord Byron written in the context of sweltering Mediterranean climate, but equally applicable to Calcutta, reads as follows:

What men call love
And the gods adultery
Is much more common
When the climate's sultry.

The early British settlers in the eighteenth century wore Indian loose-fitting and airy cotton garments at home, which were suitable for the hot climate. Later, however, in the light of increasing political power and prestige they began wearing completely unsuitable clothing designed for the English climate. Their eating and drinking habits too were not adapted to the hot climate. As a protection against the hot Indian climate, the English built their bungalows within compounds of shady trees and the rooms had very thick walls and high ceilings surrounded by covered verandas. Some wealthy high-ranking sahibs in Calcutta even maintained garden houses on the banks of the river. Some British officials in Delhi like Metcalfe and William Fraser followed the Mughal practice and built tehkhanas in their residences where they entertained their guests. Another novel feature of the English bungalows was the terrace or housetop accessible by a winding staircase from without, sometimes from within but generally from both. Colesworthy Grant in his 'An Anglo-Indian Domestic Sketch' (1849) makes a special mention of the terrace where

. . . in the cool of the evening may possibly be seen assembling the three temperaments of human life, the romping, the sentimental and the sober. It forms a playground to the first, a cool retreat and sitting room—where the veranda may not be preferred—to the last, and a promenade to the intermediate grade.

Also, many sahibs, especially bachelors, would have their cots carried to the housetop and during the hot season, with heaven as their canopy, sleep at the night. Some sahibs would set up special enclosures on the terrace and install their cots over there. Colesworthy even writes about a person known to him who slept on the bare terrace without a bed or bedding except a pillow and would remain lying there even in the rain.

We come across an interesting case of a young Company civilian who beat the heat by lying down on a cot with a mushq for a pillow and the contents of a second mushq poured over him. There were others who slept in sheets which had been previously soaked in water. As it was unbearable to sleep indoors during the hot weather some selected open spaces in their compounds. They would erect a pair of timber posts and connect their tops with a durable cross-pole carrying a hanging punkha. The cots would be brought out at night and placed under the punkha. Alongside each bed the servants would put an earthenware tub filled with water with a long-handled spoon to enable the sahibs and memsahibs to sprinkle themselves during the night without getting up.

An indigenous cooling device adopted by the sahibs was the installation of tatties made of khus-khus grass over all the openings—windows and doors—of a house. Tatties were kept continually wet by a bhishtee or a water-carrier engaged to throw water against it from outside. This was very effective in cooling when there was air, hot or cool, in the atmosphere. The rapid evaporation of sprinkled water and the refreshing odour of khus-khus made the inner spaces both cool and comfortable. The khus-khus tatties were highly valued in the upper provinces, which had hot winds, far more than in Calcutta. The use of tatties was prevalent even during Mughal times and the invention of this device is attributed to the Mughal emperor Akbar.

The punkha bears the stamp of the orient and the tropics. The use of hand punkha dates from olden times. There were many different kinds and sizes of the hand punkha. The orthodox Mughal fan consisted of a large flap, which slaves held over a grandee as he sat amidst his pile of cushions. Similar large fans used by rajas and nawabs came into usage by the British elite. Another large hand-punkha was carried by one of the bearers who accompanied the palanquin. It was made of a staff about five feet long, with a circular frame fixed to the side forming the shape of the letter P. The frame was covered with printed cloth on both sides and furnished with a full flounce about a foot in depth of the same stuff. Other hand punkhas of various dimensions were made from the branches of a palm tree. These were waved to and fro by servants called pankhawalas. There is also a mention of hand fans made of peacock tails and feathers in south India where servants also held umbrellas over their masters. All kinds of hand fans including fly switches were in common use until the last decade of the eighteenth century.

The hanging punkha, suspended from the ceiling, was introduced towards the end of the eighteenth century. Col. Yule in *Hobson-Jobson* refers to the use of this device by the Arabs, attributes its invention to Caliph Mansur (AD 753–74) and says it was known as the Marwaha al-Khaish (linen fan). There is no reference to swinging punkhas in Mughal India or in the East India Company records until 1780. William Hickey in 1785 records the luxury of hanging fans while sahibs were eating their meals. It is a French seaman, Captain de Grandpre, who first describes the Calcutta punkha in 1790.

> In many houses there was a large fan, hanging from the ceiling over the eating table, of a square form and balanced on an axle fitted to the upper part of it. A servant standing at one end of it puts it in motion by means of a cord which is fastened to it in the same manner as he would ring a bell.

Hanging punkhas are said by one authority to have been accidentally invented by a Eurasian clerk in Calcutta when he suspended the leaf of a table which was waved by a visitor to and fro resulting in a breath of cool air which suggested the idea of developing this device. The early punkhas consisted of a large wooden frame covered with cloth but later these were improved by reducing the size of the frame and enlarging the cloth flaps with frills. During the nineteenth century the fringe grew larger until the final form of a large cloth hanging from a horizontal wooden bar was reached. The size of a hanging punkha depended on the dimensions of the room. In the beginning, persons unaccustomed to the punkha sometimes complained of headaches which disappeared once after they got used to it. The ropes by which a punkha was suspended had to be regularly checked to prevent accidents of its falling down and hurting those sitting below or damaging the furniture on the floor.

The installation of punkhas in lecture halls and other public places was often advertised to attract visitors. We also come across amusing accounts of waving punkhas in the church when some memsahibs complained that their bonnets were swept by the punkhas pulled by different men who kept different time creating confusion. Earlier, the man pulling the punkha would stand in the room but later the device of passing the cord through a hole in the wall was resorted to which enabled the punkhawalla (rope-puller) to sit or lie on the floor outside and not disturb the privacy of the sahibs. As time passed punkhas became popular with the Europeans in Bombay, Madras and elsewhere in the country. In many houses, punkhas were fixed not only in sitting and dining rooms but also in the sleeping apartments suspended over the beds to be used throughout the night. In the latter half of the nineteenth century there was ornamentation of punkhas with paintings in pleasing designs or covering with coloured cloth with broad frills.

Besides the punkha, there was another mostly forgotten device used in some British homes for beating the heat called the 'thermantidote'. It was a huge box containing a revolving hand-operated fan, like a steam boat paddle, with tatties-fitted windows on each side. The hot air sucked in by this gadget would pass through moist tatties, filling the entire house with cool air bringing solace to the memsahib who would write home about various modes of cooling during the ghastly Indian summer. There is a mention of this novel device in the writings of Fanny Parks in 1831. This invention is attributed to Dr George Green Spilsbury who came to India in 1823 and was for some years surgeon to the Saugor Political Agency.

Before the introduction of ice, an important servant of the sahib's household was the abdar entrusted with the job of cooling the water, wines, beer and other table delicacies, which depended more for value and acceptance on their refreshing coolness than their flavour. The abdar was the walking refrigerator of those days and went with his master to every dinner party for cooling the master's wine, using saltpetre in a container for the bottle.

The introduction of American ice in 1833 brought great jubilation and feasting in Calcutta. It replaced mountain ice, brought down at heavy cost and inconvenience, and other native ice which would be produced in ice pits during winter nights and preserved for the summer, entailing colossal wastage. Small earthen pots filled with water would be placed in an open field and in the morning the coating of ice formed in the cold temperature of the night would be collected and stored in ice pits. It was after over twenty years of experimenting in the early nineteenth century that an American entrepreneur Fredrick Tudor succeeded in transporting ice from a cold to a hot climate. The ice blocks cut from the frozen ponds rented near Boston were stored in an ice house before loading them on board a ship which had an in-built ice house. The first shipment of American ice arrived in Calcutta in September 1833 by S.S. *Tussany* after a four-month voyage around the Cape. Wrapped in felt and pine sawdust, two-thirds of the ice cargo in solid form was received with great excitement. So much so that Governor General Lord Bentinck presented an inscribed silver-gilt cup to the ship's captain William C. Rogers for having successfully landed the first shipment of American ice in India. This encouraged the exporter Fredrick Tudor to make ice shipments to Bombay and Madras also. Ice houses were soon constructed in all three ports to store the precious ice cargo and preserve it against heat. There was a growing demand for this crystal-clear ice among the local European population and wealthy Indians. Selling at four annas a seer, half the price of native ice, it became popular with everyone who could afford it. Tudor in turn made a fortune through this ice trade for over thirty years until the technology of making ice was introduced in India.

Another useful device which served as a shield against the killer sun of the tropics was the sola topi. There is no authentic record of when and who invented it but the first mention of the sola topi appears in Fanny Parks's *Wanderings of a Pilgrim* when she writes about some robbery in 1833. The sola topi took many years before it came into common use. People had used various kinds of head covering for protection against the sun's rays. It was after 1857 that the sola topi attained its supremacy and pushed out all other kinds of sun hats. The popular version was made of pith and covered with khaki cloth with overhangs at the front and back to shade the eyes and neck from the direct rays of the sun. It became a symbol of imperial might as no sahib ever appeared in public without a hat. They wore them even during rain and some sahibs got them enamelled to turn them waterproof.

After consolidating their hold on major parts of India the British created their 'little Englands' with English-style cottages in the hill stations. With their cool climate, lush greenery and glorious views of snow-covered peaks, they offered an escape from the grilling heat of the plains. Simla, the pride of the Raj, became the summer capital of India from 1830, followed by Ooty for Madras, Nainital for Lucknow, Mahabaleshwar for Bombay and Darjeeling for Calcutta. With their holiday atmosphere, picnics and parties, the hill stations provided a refuge for the invalid and the bored and a fun place for pleasure-seeking sahibs and memsahibs. Emily Eden, sister of Governor General Auckland described Simla as 'the nearest place to dear home that one could hope for in this dreadful country'. From 1864 Simla became the seat of government from April to October and the ruling elite and their staff would move en block from Calcutta to run the administration from there. With Kipling's writings, Simla acquired a further reputation for merriment, gaiety, high living and not-so-harmless flirting. Nevertheless, the hill stations became popular especially with memsahibs who supposedly wilted under the heat much more rapidly than their menfolk.

17

Sahibs and the Brahmin Who
Knew Tomorrow

Astrology has wielded either a pervasive or a peripheral influence in many civilizations, both ancient and modern. As a story goes, Nobel laureate C.V. Raman was once performing religious rituals with offerings of food to his ancestors in Gaya when someone said to him, 'Sir, you are such a great scientist—how can you believe this food would reach your ancestors?' Sir Raman smiled and replied, 'I cannot prove that it will not reach them.'

The pursuit of knowledge demands banishment of preconceived notions and prejudices. The universe is full of mysteries, and faith in the supernatural teaches man that he knows much less than he thinks. We should have an open mind on all questions and also keep alive our spirit of inquiry. Recently there have been attempts in the West to re-establish a sound theoretical basis for astrology but such attempts have not yet achieved any conclusive results. However, there is no doubt about the popularity of astrology all over the world. It is estimated that more than half the world's population either believes in it or is interested enough to consult astrologers and read predictions published in the media.

In India, the Vedic period witnessed a remarkable flowering of astrology. There is a vast amount of Sanskrit literature on the subject, explaining the complex system and techniques evolved over centuries by learned sages and philosophers. Greek astrology was also transmitted to India through some Sanskrit translations in the second and third centuries AD. But the techniques of Indian astrology were related to divine revelations and the Hindu doctrine of the transmigration of souls. The role of karma, the Indian theory of five elements (i.e., earth, water, air, fire and space) and the Hindu system of values were also incorporated into the study of astrology.

The second half of the eighteenth century saw the flowering of British interest in India's history, literature, and civilization. This was the time when Sir William Jones established the Asiatic Society, scholars like Colebrook and Wilson translated Sanskrit classics, and James Forbes produced his monumental *Oriental Memoirs* (1813). An eminent Company official who spent nearly twenty years in India (1765–84), Forbes, wrote about his encounter with a brahmin astrologer who startled him with his amazing prophesies.

Forbes speaks about some brahmins who, like the magicians of Egypt and the astrologers of Chaldea, were supposed to 'have within them the spirit of the holy gods, and light and understanding, and wisdom in showing hard sentences and dissolving of doubts'. Different from the common soothsayers and astrologers found everywhere in India, this special class of brahmins was gifted with a talent marked by deep learning. Forbes met one of this class who was well known to his circle of friends and colleagues. He relates three episodes in confirmation of the penetrating vision of this brahmin whose predictions came true.

The first one relates to the appointment of the governor of Bombay in place of Mr Crommelin who was under orders of transfer back home in January 1767. When Forbes arrived there in 1766 he learnt that Mr Spencer, the second in council had been appointed Crommelin's successor in the Bombay government. But the English community was divided into three parties: one that paid its court to Spencer, the rising sun; another gratefully adhered to Crommelin; and the third was affectionately devoted to the interest of Hodges, whom they considered to have been deprived of his just right as successor to Crommelin. Crommelin had gone out as a writer to Bombay in 1732, Hodges in 1737 and Spencer in 1741.

At that time supersession in the Company's service was little known; faithful service and a fair character, if life was spared, generally met with reward. Previous to Lord Clive being appointed governor of Bengal, in 1764, Spencer had been removed from Bombay to Calcutta, and for some time he had acted as the provisional governor of Bengal. On Lord Clive's nomination to the Government of Bengal, Spencer was appointed by the court of directors to return to Bombay, with the rank of second in council, and an order to succeed Mr Crommelin in January 1767. This supersession and appointment was deemed an act of injustice by the Company's civil servants in general, and as personal injury by Mr Hodges in particular, who was then chief of Surat, second in council, and next in regular succession to the Government of Bombay, which he looked upon as his right, being senior to Mr Spencer by four years.

In his frustration Hodges addressed a spirited letter from Surat to the governor and council, complaining of injustice in the court of directors, with whom, as an individual, he was not permitted to correspond. The governor and council of Bombay deeming his letter improper and disrespectful to his employers, ordered him to reconsider it and make a suitable apology; this not being complied with, he was removed from his post as chief of Surat, and suspended from the Company's service.

The learned brahmin knew Hodges from his younger days in the service and they were good friends. The brahmin had assured Hodges that he would gradually rise from the station he then held at Cambay, to other higher appointments as chief at Tellicherry and Surat, and would close his Indian career by being governor of Bombay.

Hodges spoke of these brahminical predictions among his associates and friends from their very first communication; and their author was generally called Mr Hodges's brahmin. However, these predictions for some years made but little impression on Hodges's mind. Afterwards, as he successively ascended the gradations in the Company's service, he placed more confidence in his brahmin, especially when he approached near the pinnacle of ambition and found himself chief of Surat, the next situation in wealth and honour to the governorship of Bombay. When, therefore, Spencer was appointed governor and Hodges suspended from service, he sent for his brahmin and told him about his situation and impending departure for England. He even slightly reproached him for having deceived him by false promises. The brahmin coolly replied, 'You see this veranda, and the apartment to which it leads; Mr Spencer has reached the portico, but he will not enter the palace. He has set his foot upon the threshold, but he shall not enter into the house! Notwithstanding all appearances to the contrary, you will attain the honours I foretold, and fill the high station to which he has been appointed. A dark cloud is before him!'

This singular prophecy was publicly known in Surat and Bombay; and the truth or falsehood of the brahmin was the subject of discussion in every company. Hodges's faith in his prediction seemed to have had very little influence on his conduct; for, in obedience to the orders of his superiors, he had returned from Surat to Bombay, and was preparing for his voyage to Europe. Then suddenly in November 1766, an express communication arrived from England via the overland route and then by sea from Basra to Bombay. There was a letter from the court of directors to the president and council, in answer to their representation about Hodges's conduct, mentioning, in the first place, that on a review of Spencer's proceedings while he was the governor of Bengal, he appeared so blameable that they had thought proper to annul his appointment to the Government of Bombay, dismiss him from the Company's service, and order him to proceed to England without delay.

Although the conduct of Mr Hodges had been improper they were pleased to pass it over; and, in consideration of his long and faithful services, his good character and well-known abilities, they had taken off his suspension, and ordered him to succeed to the Government of Bombay on Mr Crommelin's transfer in the month of January 1767. So Spencer embarked for England finally in December; and Mr Crommelin sailed in January, leaving Hodges in complete possession of the government. Thereafter Hodges developed such a deep faith and respect for his brahmin friend that as the governor of Bombay he undertook no important step without consulting him.

The second episode relates to the same brahmin and was as well known in Bombay as the former. When Forbes first arrived in Bombay to join as a writer in the Company, he met a very kind-hearted gentleman who introduced him to his family and treated him as one of his family members. The lady of the house had been a widow when she had married this gentleman. Her first husband had died when she was very young, leaving two children, a son and a daughter. The latter remained with her mother, the former was sent to England for education, and at the age of sixteen embarked for Bombay with the appointment of a writer, some years prior to Forbes's arrival there. The ships of that season all reached Bombay in safety, except the one in which this young gentleman sailed, which at length was taken as lost.

A mother could not so easily give up hope and her usual evening walk was on a sandy beach, forming a bay in full view of the ocean. The shore of that bay was also a cremation place for the Hindus where brahmins assembled for the ceremony, and Hodges' brahmin, then at Bombay, was occasionally among them.

Observing the mother's anxiety, he asked her the cause; the lady being a native of India, inquired in his own language why a man so extraordinarily gifted should be ignorant of her sad situation. The brahmin was moved and said, 'I do know the reason of your sorrow; your son lives; the ship will soon arrive in safety, but you will never more behold him!' She immediately mentioned this conversation to her friends. A signal was given to locate the missing ship. It was traced but her son had remained in Brazil, where the ship having been long detained for repair, the Jesuits had converted this promising youth to the church of Rome. Instead of conducting him to his mother, they only delivered her letters full of affectionate entreaties that she should follow his example, and enter into the true church. Her son stayed on at Rio de Janeiro, and occasionally wrote to her, but after the suppression of the Jesuits with many other members of that society, he was sent from South America to the prisons of Portugal, and no more heard of.

His sister, who remained with her mother at Bombay, married a gentleman in the Company's civil service, by whom she had a large family. Her sudden demise in England where she had gone to supervise the education of her children brought another terrible blow to the mother. Not long after this event, an intimate friend of the family, on a visit to Lisbon, found the long-lost son in a prison there. The information about the young man was conveyed to London immediately and official steps were taken to restore the young man to his mother. This extraordinary news did shed a momentary gleam of joy on her countenance, but it was soon succeeded by renewed pangs of sorrow, and a continued exclamation of 'O the brahmin! The brahmin!'

Her husband endeavoured to rouse her from melancholy by assurances that every difficulty was removed, that the Almighty having infinite wisdom thought proper to deprive her of one child, had mercifully restored another in this unexpected manner, whom she had long considered dead. All seemed to produce no effect, even on a religious mind, of which resignation and indifference seemed to have taken mingled possession. Every prospect set before her of future joy and comfort only produced a monotonous repetition of 'The brahmin! The brahmin!'

The friend at Lisbon, when all was happily accomplished, lost no time in communicating to her son that his mother lived, was married to a gentleman of fortune and respectability, and both were waiting to welcome him under their parental roof and that he had come to take him from a scene of misery to life, light, and joy.

Although the communication was made in the most considerate manner, the sudden transition seemed too much for human nature. The son's spirit failed, for he believed it not or scarcely believed the reality of his emancipation from those dreary walls where he had for years been debarred from the light of the sun and fresh air. The sudden transition from hopeless despair in the dungeon's gloom to the sight of the sun, the fanning of the breeze, and the sympathy of friendship were too much for his emaciated frame. He faintly uttered the effusions of a grateful heart, and expired. Thus was the brahmin's prediction to his mother, uttered a full thirty years before, completely fulfilled.

The third episode refers to a young gentleman and his wife with a child who arrived in Bombay from England. Having been appointed to a Company's post at Surat, he proceeded there leaving his wife with a friend's family until he had procured a house, and made suitable provisions for her reception at Surat. On the eve of her departure for Surat, the same brahmin astrologer happened to visit her host family in Bombay. The host who was holding a high position introduced him to the company, and in a sort of jest asked him to tell the destiny of the happy, fair one lately arrived from Europe. To the surprise of the whole company, and particularly to the surprise of the object of inquiry, he gave her a penetrating and compassionate look; and after a solemn pause, said to the gentleman in the native language, 'Her cup of felicity is full, but evanescent. A bitter potion awaits her; for which she must prepare.'

Her husband had written that he would come in a barge to Surat to accompany her on shore. He did not appear; but a friend of his went on board to inform her of his dangerous illness; he was then in the last paroxysm of a fever, and expired in her arms.

Forbes, after citing these cases, pays tribute to the ancient wisdom of 'Hindustan, where arts and science, learning and philosophy and the sublimest poetry were encouraged by the native sovereigns at a time when Greece and Rome were involved in darkness, and Egypt herself was probably in a state of comparative barbarism.' He adds: 'The Mahomedan conquests and other causes have sadly degraded not only the philosophy and science of the Hindoos, but totally destroyed the simplicity of a religion which there can be no doubt was then essentially different from modern brahminism. If there should still remain any of that priesthood who adore God in his unity, and cherish the sublime ideas then inculcated, it is perhaps not easy to determine the limits of their researchers, or the gifts and talents they possess.'

18

Sadhus, Sufis and Sanyasis

Saintliness through the ages has been prized as the supreme virtue in India. Sanyasis, yogis and vairagis belonged to a class of Hindu ascetics or sadhus who renounced worldly pleasures and desires and through austere penances tried to attain the highest religious merit and spiritual bliss. Among Muslims, the dervish was the ideal, and Sufi saints and fakirs, likewise, gave up all earthly attachments. They were greatly venerated and taken care of by the people at large as a religious duty. They travelled far and wide and visited holy cities, sacred mountains and rivers, temples and mosques. Endowed with powers of blessing and cursing, they were held in great esteem. European travellers and visitors were struck by the image of these holy men who were considered 'the outward and visible signs of India's inward spiritual grace of vivid realization of the higher world in which all things live, and move, and have their being'.

Hindu ascetics belonged to different categories or groups. There were sanyasis who had renounced all sensual pleasures and carnal appetites, took to fasting and abstinence and stayed away from their kith and kin. Next came the yogis who practised yoga along with prayers, holding their breath for a long time and making their souls flee and wander in the cosmos and even enter the body of a dying person. They were believed to have life spans of hundreds of years. The vairagis belonged to the Hindu monastic order who worshipped Lord Vishnu while the gosains were devotees of the great Lord Shiva. But the usual general term for all these Hindu ascetics is sadhu which means a pious and holy man 'who has forsaken all things except that spark of Divine which is Himself'. For him 'all things are maya or illusion'. The secret of life is how to escape from life.

Nineteenth-century accounts mention numerous ascetic sects and establishments supported by charities and landed endowments. Members of these sects lived under the spiritual guidance of their gurus, the heads of these institutions. Most of them were serious mendicants undertaking study of the scriptures and imparting knowledge of religious duties to the common people. Among the Muslims also there were several orders of Sufis and fakirs whose members practised severe penance and emotional, ecstatic modes of worship like those of the Hindus.

There are references to various modes of self-torture and mortification undertaken by sadhus for the expiation of all sins and attainment of spiritual bliss. James Forbes records in his *Memoirs*:

> Some of them enter into a solemn vow to continue for life in one unvaried posture; others undertake to carry a cumbrous load, or drag a heavy chain; some crawl on their hands and knees, for years, around an extensive empire; and others roll their bodies on the earth, from the shores of the Indus to the banks of the Ganges and

in that humiliating posture, collect money to enable them either to build a temple or dig a well, or atone for some particular sin. Some swing during their whole life, in this torrid clime, before a slow fire; others suspend themselves, with their head downwards, for a certain time, over the fiercest flames.

I have seen a man who had made a vow to hold up his arms in a perpendicular manner above his head, and never to suspend them; at length he totally lost the power of moving them at all. He was one of the gymnosophists, who wear no kind of covering, and seemed more like a wild beast than a man; his arms, from having been so long in one posture, were withered, and dried up; while his outstretched fingers, with long nails of twenty years growth, gave them the appearance of extraordinary horns; his hair, full of dust and never combed, hung over him in a savage manner; and, except in his erect posture, there appeared nothing human about him. This man was travelling throughout Hindostan, and being unable to help himself with food, women of distinction among the Hindoos contended for the honour of feeding this holy person wherever he appeared.

I saw another of these devotees, who was one of the phallic worshippers of Seeva; and who, not content with wearing or adorning the symbol of that deity, had made a vow to fix every year a large iron ring into the most tender part of his body, and thereto suspend a heavy chain, many yards long, to drag on the ground. I saw this extraordinary saint, in the seventh year of penance, when he had just put in the seventh ring and the wound was then so recent and painful, that he was obliged to carry the chain upon his shoulder until the orifice became more callous.

Sadhus lived in caves or under banyan trees near temples and shrines. In the south, Pundarams, their bodies smeared with ashes, went about singing hymns with alms bowls. Although a great number of them were really genuine and zealous ascetics, there were some impostors as well who roamed about for a free subsistence.

According to Martyn, the uncritical charity in the name of religion encouraged mendicancy in the lower classes, and fakirs and vairagis of doubtful religious merits swarmed the entire social polity. Stavorinus describes some of them going entirely naked and carrying a thick club, with their bodies smeared with ash. Some Europeans dismissed them as ignorant savages or half-crazy fanatics. Flora Annie Steel, the famous writer, however, observed in the 1890s:

> They are neither; they are extremely well-educated, deeply versed in metaphysics and speculative lore, with a dialectic skill which is surprising. Some of them—these naked savages—will astonish you by quoting Herbert Spencer, for even nowadays they are recruited from all classes, and they belong by rights to the most thoughtful of each class. In the West the thinker becomes an agnostic, or a parson or a philanthropist; in India—he becomes a Sadhu.

Steele adds:

> Up in the mountain wilderness of Kashmir among the Eternal Snows, you may come upon a man who has journeyed on foot almost from Cape Comorin, who has slept out under the stars, who has passed through the world, as it were and carried nothing with him, save the one Divine spark which he seeks to unite once more with the Great Mystery which lies behind all worlds. Many of these Yogis are mighty thinkers. The fineness of their philosophical reasonings, the subtlety of their dialectics leave one amazed.

Some sadhus were credited with miraculous powers, acquired through self-torture undertaken to gain spiritual ascendancy over themselves and others. The Reverend Butler writes about a sadhu who took it into his head after long years of austerities that he could exalt himself by riding about in a sort of sedan chair with the seat stuck with nails. He was carried from town to town. There was great admiration for his endurance everywhere.

According to William Sleeman (1844) Indian sadhus were in general exceedingly intelligent men of the world, very communicative, and some came from the most wealthy families. One happened to visit his district and it was discovered that he was the son of his friend, a rich landlord, having left his home twelve years before. He joined his family on the pleadings of his mother but disappeared again after about a year.

Generally speaking, asceticism was not recommended for women. Female devotees are, however, mentioned but people did not show much reverence for them. Saints and sadhus did not normally enrol them as disciples. Some widows at times joined groups of pilgrims and visited holy places.

Associated with religion, astrology was recognized as a noble profession. A general belief that the planets and their movements governed the lives of mortals prevailed over Hindus and Muslims alike. All classes of people, including Europeans, consulted Indian astrologers and believed in their predictions. Through astrology people explored the prospects of their health, wealth and material prosperity. Every venture, activity, and even a journey, were undertaken on the advice of astrologers to ascertain the auspiciousness of the day and time.

Indian astrologers assigned the days of the week to different planets. Each planet exercised its influence on people and events during the space of a year. Dubois describes the principles on which astrologers calculated the influence of celestial bodies. According to him, astrology was 'a science which opens so vast a sphere to the imagination'. Undoubtedly in India, it was raised to the status of a science, almost precise. Horoscopes were drawn up on the basis of time and place of birth and the position of planets at that moment. These were believed to be sure guides to determine the course of life.

19

Encounters with Snakes

Legends of wonder, fear and veneration inspired by snakes are told all over the world. Anecdotes of Indian snakes and snake charmers abound in foreign accounts of India and scholars studied mythological tales of snakes and the origin of serpent worship. There are also graphic descriptions of their encounters with different kinds of snakes especially the *cobra de capello* or hooded snake (nag). Credit also goes to an English doctor, Patrick Russel, for a pioneering scientific study of Indian serpents (1796), the various species, poisonous and non-poisonous, their curious behaviour patterns during different seasons and the remedies for snakebites.

British settlers lived in continued dread of snakes lurking in houses, gardens and camps, even on roads. Several devices were used to keep snakes out of homes but they still managed to find their way in, sometimes darting out from the roof, or getting underfoot. They coiled in bookshelves, crawled down verandahs, rested on beds or hid in creepers and made their way through drains which were dry and uncovered by the road.

A favourite haunt of snakes was the bathroom, and there were occasions when memsahibs had the horrible experience of sitting in their tin bathtubs while a cobra coolly surveyed the scene. The Rev. Acland wrote in his journal:

> So great is the dread of snakes here, that no one even sleeps without a light, lest stepping out of bed at night, he should place his foot on some venomous creature; most people keep a long bamboo in every room. We never put on our shoes without first examining well, that there is nothing alive in them.

A nineteenth-century humorous verse 'As Wise As A Serpent' in the *Lays of Ind* describes a sahib's tête-à-tête with a cobra in his bathroom:

From time immemorial men have agreed
That serpents are very cute creatures indeed.

. . .

I propose to narrate a remarkable case,
which happened quite lately before my own house:

. . .

Well I sat in the water and revelled, and rolled
Through my heat-thirsty pores deep inhaling the cold,
Dashing it down on my head in my face,
With a whoop and a splashing all over the place,
When—and just at the 'moment supreme' of my joys—
I heard, 'neath the tub a peculiar noise.

The sound was a sound which makes guinea-pigs quake,
And men for the matter of that. 'Twas a snake.
Slowly from under the tub he appeared,

Hissing; then stopped and his angry crest roared;
And I cannot declare I felt eased in mind
When I saw 'twas a cobra of deadliest kind.

He sat there, erect, wide expanding his hood,
As if he'd get at me if only he could;
But I stuck to my tub, and its lifty green side
Was a bulwark from which his assault I defied.

An impulse heroic coursed swift through my veins
To give that old cobra a dance for his pains,
From my tub like a burglar I noiselessly stept,
Like an Indian stalking a chicken I crept,
With a grin of delight, I believe, on each feature,
At thinking what glory to diddle the creature.

I stood by the hold—I stood over his tail;
I seized it, and hauled as you'd haul at a sail.
He wriggled and hissed with a horrible sound,
But the hole was so small that he couldn't turn
round;
So I held him there writhing, and laughed as he tried,
Half his length in the bathroom the other outside.

Mrs Clemons in her journal (1841) recounts a rare
incident when her friend Mrs S discovered a large snake
coiled up under the mattress of the palanquin after she
had slept soundly upon it for three hours, during a
march of eleven miles.

Daniel Johnson, a surgeon in a Calcutta hospital
(1820s), who carried out many experiments with snakes,
describes how, while sleeping in the open air under the
thatch of a house, he was bitten by a snake which had
crawled on to his bed. He took a full bottle of Madeira
and ran up and down until he was quite exhausted. The
snake was not venomous and he recovered duly.

We come across the case of another company official who was obsessed with keeping snakes and tried to domesticate them. The snake catchers used to bring him every variety of species after extracting their fangs. One day, he was feeding his snakes with milk when one of them suddenly turned up and bit him on the hand. On examining the snake he found that one of the fangs had grown back and that venom was secreted from it. He had it immediately killed, together with the whole tribe of his favourites, but it was too late, for he died in the course of two days in spite of all the medical aid given to him at Madras.

Many sahibs were led to believe that the sound of music worked powerfully on snakes. Snakes, they believed, were induced to come out of hiding, to be caught or killed, and that the snake charmer could tame serpents especially the cobra and make them dance to the melody of his gourd pipe. James Forbes (c.1800) made an extraordinary drawing of a cobra, the most venomous of the species. He writes that he painted it while:

> . . . it danced for an hour on the table during which I frequently handled it, to observe the beauty of the spots and especially the spectacles on the hood, not doubting but that its venomous fangs had been previously extracted.

Forbes had a miraculous escape—the next morning he was told that the same snake had bitten a woman who died within half an hour of being bitten. About the dancing cobras, he adds that the snake charmers:

> . . . play a few simple notes on the flute, with which the snakes seem much delighted, and keep time by a graceful motion of the die head, erecting about half their length

from the ground and following the music with the gentle curves, like the undulating lines of swans' necks.

When the music ceased the snakes would become motionless and be consigned to their baskets.

Captain Charles Gold (1790) was convinced that music had considerable power over snakes, as he saw them rising from their baskets and turning towards the instrument to the sound of music with distended hoods. They continued with an easy motion of their heads, in a manner dancing while the tune lasted and then coiled themselves up again.

Another observer noted:

> It is really strange, but it is a fact that the cobra is attracted by music . . . I was once playing upon my harp in an open verandah that led into the garden by a few steps; a snake had reached the second step, and lay there for some time unperceived. A gentleman entered the garden and saw it and bid me by signs to play on. I did so for a few minutes, during which time, the snake remained perfectly still. I then left off, when it immediately raised its head . . . and took refuge in the neighbouring bush. The gentleman begged me to resume my harp in order to allure the deadly foe to its own destruction. This I did; the music produced the same effect as before and the poor creature was shortly killed.

In his treatise on Indian snakes (1874), Edward Nicholson points out on the other hand that the music played by snake charmers during the cobra's performance was quite superfluous. The very imperfect condition of the auditory apparatus would suggest that it is highly probable that far from enjoying music the snake has very little appreciation of sound. To support this he cites the Burmese who put a cobra through the same performance without the aid of music and also without extracting its fangs, a precaution generally taken by Indian snake charmers.

Associated with gods, snakes were traditionally worshipped. It was difficult to find an orthodox Hindu willing to kill a snake. Edwin Arnold (1900) says:

> You may see a cobra regularly domiciled in an Indian hut, inhabiting either the roof or the foundation, quite undisturbed by the family . . . he appears and disappears doing no injury except to the rats and the people will set a daily bowl of milk for him and call him 'Uncle'. However if in the dark anyone tread upon him his bite would be a certain death.

It is believed that snakes are gifted and that they have strong affections. The male serpent is smaller and brighter in colour than the female and stays beside its dead 'wife', if not disturbed, for days together. Even in captivity they learn to distinguish persons and get attached to those who show affinity.

John Lockwood Kipling summed up the traditional Indian attitude to the cobra:

> He is the necklace of the gods, he can give gems to the poor, he is guardian of priceless treasures, he can change himself into manifold forms, he casts his skin annually—and thus has the gift of youth . . . he is in the confidence and counsel of gods and demons, and when the great world was made, he was already there.

Snake charmers followed a hereditary calling. Wrapped in mystery and romance, they kept up traditions of a remote past. Beholding them and their dancing snakes, one felt there was a mysterious tie between the serpent and his master who was privy to an inexplicable power over his serpents, and the seductive tunes of the gourd pipe exercised an uncanny influence over them.

There are several accounts describing the snake-charmer's method of catching snakes. The process involved his playing his pipe in the neighbourhood where a snake had been sighted. Drawn by the music, the snake would come out and make its appearance. The charmer would seize the reptile by the point of the tail with his left hand and slip the right hand along the body with the swiftness of lightning. Then grasping him by the throat with his finger and thumb, he would force him to open his jaws and display his poisonous fangs. Once trapped, the fangs would be extracted, and the charmer would take him away for taming. There were instances when it came to light that a snake that came out at the sound of his music was a tame one deprived of its fangs and hidden by the snake charmer for the purpose of demonstrating his powers to the spectators.

The largest of the serpents is the python or boa constrictor. Travellers have left authentic accounts about the great power and dimensions of this creature. It was said to have the capacity of devouring complete buffaloes and cows after crushing them within the voluminous coil of its tail. It would usually suspend itself by the tail from the branch of a large tree, dropping with the velocity of a thunder upon goats, deer, buffaloes, men and even tigers, or indeed any animal except the elephant that may chance to come within its reach. The sound of its hissing was loud enough to be audible at a great distance and the sweep of its tail so terrible that plants and trees fell beneath its force as if blown by a cannon shot.

The Rev. Caunter in his journal (1838) describes an

English army officer's encounter near Dindigul with a gigantic boa over fifty feet long and a full three in circumference, moving in a deep recess of a ruined monument. The officer and his soldiers armed with bayonets launched an attack on this enormous serpent, but it uncoiled itself in a few seconds and such was its prodigious strength that with one mighty sweep of its tail, it dashed five of its assailants to the earth. The sixth, who was near its head maintained his position and continued his attack until the animal, exhausted with pain and exertion, lay motionless. By this time, the five soldiers, who had been struck down, having recovered, killed the vanquished snake.

Almost every foreign visitor to India was entertained by an exhibition of dancing snakes by the charmers. Abbe Dubois, the French missionary who spent thirty years in India from 1792, wrote a detailed account on the performance of snake charmers. He was fascinated by their most alarming tricks with these deadly reptiles. A favourite trick was to make the dried skin of the cobra alive. Drew Gay, the *Telegraph* correspondent, was amazed on seeing this performance. He noted, 'You may examine the apparatus closely every time and watch the operation as carefully as you please, yet you cannot detect the *modus operandi*.'

Another startling feat performed at Fort William in Calcutta, the conversion of a brass coin into a snake, is thus described by W.H. Carey:

> The juggler gave me a coin to hold, and then seated himself about five yards from me, on a small rug from which he never attempted to move during the whole performance. I showed the coin to several persons who were close beside me, on a form in front of the juggler.

At a sign from him, I not only grasped the coin I held firmly in my right hand, I enclosed them both as firmly as I could between my knees. Of course, I was positively certain that the small coin was within my double fists.

The juggler then began a sort of incantation, accompanied by a monotonous and discordant kind of a recitative, and repeated the words Ram Shambhu during some minutes. He then suddenly stopped and, still keeping his seat, made a quick motion with his right hand, as if throwing something at me, giving at the same time a puff with his mouth. At that instant I felt my hands suddenly distend, and become partly open, while I experienced a sensation as if a cold ball of dough, or something equally soft, nasty, and disagreeable was now between my palms. I stared to my feet in astonishment, also to the astonishment of others, and opening my hands, found there no coin, but to my horror and alarm (for all created things I detest and loathe the genus), I saw a young snake, all alive—oh! and of all snakes in the world, a *cobra de capello*, folded or rather coiled roundly up. I threw it instantly to the ground, trembling with rage and fear, as if already bitten by the deadly reptile; which began immediately to crawl along the ground, to the alarm and amazement of everyone present.

The juggler now got up for the first time since he had sat down, and catching hold of the snake displayed its length, which was nearly two feet—two feet all but an inch and a half. He then took it cautiously by the tail, and opening his own mouth to its widest extent, let the head of the snake drop into it, and deliberately commenced to swallow the animal till the end of the tail only was visible; then making a sudden gulp, the whole of the snake was apparently swallowed. After this, he came up to the spectators, and opening his mouth wide, permitted us to look into his throat, but no snake or snake's tail was visible, it was seemingly down his throat altogether. During the remainder of the performances, we never saw this snake again, nor did the man profess of his ability to make it reappear, but he performed another snake-trick, which surprised us very much. He took from a bag another *cobra de capello*, and walking into the centre of the room, enclosed it in his hands in a folded state. He waved, or shook them for some time in this condition, and then opened his fists, when, hey! presto!—the snake was gone, and in its place appeared several small ones, which he suffered to fall from his hands, when they glided, with their peculiar undulating movement, almost like the waves of the sea, about the floor.

The French traveller, Louis Rousselet (1860s) was taken aback by another trick, which bore a striking resemblance to the famous miracle of Moses before Pharaoh, the conversion of a wand into a snake. The snake charmer held a flexible wand which he whirled for some minutes above his head and suddenly flung at our feet, where it arrived in the form of a serpent.

> In spite of the closest attention on two repetitions of this feat, I could not detect the moment when the wand was exchanged for the serpent. The trick is executed so rapidly that credulous people would swear the transformation was real.

As regards remedies for snakebite, the charmers claimed to have a special snake stone which if placed over the bitten part could suck the poison and save the life of a victim. Mrs Clemons in her journal supports the version, and noted that the stone, after its application to the snakebite, was placed in a basin of milk and it emitted some yellowish liquid which proved to be poison. Many others, however, dismissed it as worthless. Some snake catchers in Karnataka were reported to possess a medicine which secured them from the effects of venom. It was found to be effective in some cases, but no monetary temptation could induce them to part with the recipe. There was another antidote called the Tanjore Pill which had been used with some success. According to the Rev. Acland (1842):

> The only possible cure and that is an uncertain one is to swallow every few minutes a glass of brandy with eau-de-luce or smelling salts dissolved in it, while a man stands near, beating you with a heavy whip or instead of this you may be fastened to a carriage and be compelled to run as fast as possible. The object is to keep you awake, for the danger of the bite is the heavy lethargy it produces.

On learning that a mongoose is the natural enemy of snakes and could fight and kill them, many Englishmen kept them as pets at home. H.M. Kisch, a young civilian in the 1870s, gives a graphic account of a genuine battle between a mongoose and a snake which he arranged to witness by paying the price for the snake that was killed. He kept four mongooses as pets that would run around his house peeping into every hole and corner and scare away the snakes.

The annual Indian mortality from snakebite was estimated at around 20,000 in 1870. As Englishmen always wore shoes and had their feet and legs covered, they seldom, if ever, got bitten by snakes. It was the barefoot native who suffered by treading unintentionally upon a coiled serpent. According to the records of the British army in India during 1860–71, there were only four deaths during these twelve years from snakebites but thirty-eight from dog bites.

In the late nineteenth century, the government launched a drive for the extermination of serpents by offering rewards to the catchers of venomous snakes. The number of snakes brought in for reward increased so much that the initial prize of eight annas per piece was reduced to three annas, but still they came. The experiment was a failure and its was realized that government funds should rather be used for the improvement of health and medical facilities for the people and prevention of epidemics such as cholera and plague. The snake scheme was therefore given up as an 'absurd exercise'.

20

Fairs and Festivals

Religious festivities have always been a delightful diversion in the lives of Indians. Festivals give intensity to community life, inspire hilarity, feasting and social contact on a large scale, with people spending lavishly, far beyond their means, on these celebrations. English visitors were greatly impressed by the hectic gaiety of the native people, singing and dancing with their drums at village fairs and festivals. The festivities included puppet shows, pantomimes and nautches, and have been exquisitely described by men and women authors. As we go through their accounts and see visual records of the events left by professional and amateur artists, the whole scene appears to us like a pageant. We also find evidence of cordiality between the Hindus and Muslims with fervent participation in each other's festivals. To the foreigner, these occasions provided the ideal opportunity for social intercourse with Indians and observing their traits and characteristics. Festivals described include the major Hindu and Muslim celebrations, such as the Holi, Diwali, Durga Puja, Janmashtami, Muharram and the

Id. Among the regional events, a great deal has been written about Charak Puja or hook swinging, a form of ritual self-mortification.

The Hindu festival of spring Holi was easily the most popular for its colour, fun and laughter. It had a special attraction for the sahibs. An ancient festival, in early times it was celebrated in honour of Kama, the god of love, and to express the passion inspired by spring. It was later observed during Mughal times and called Id-i-Gulabi or Ab-i-Pashi. Omrahs and nobles gave rose-water bottles to one another and there was much merriment with dance and music. Holi also marked the commencement of the new year and both Hindus and Muslims hailed it amidst hysterical rejoicing with drums, singing and dancing. The nawab of Awadh, like the later Mughal emperors, continued the tradition of Akbar's time of celebrating Hindu festivals in his court. Mir Taqi Mir (1722–1808), one of the greatest Urdu poets, hailed in beautiful verses the celebration of Holi in Awadh in which nawabs themselves participated. Holi was also portrayed as a feast in honour of Lord Krishna and his dalliance with the gopis. Images of the deity were carried about on elephants, horses, and in palanquins in processions with the multitude singing in praise of Krishna and hailing the arrival of spring. British accounts of Holi describe it as a carnival of the Hindus, a sort of Hindu saturnalia, a time of universal merriment and joy and licence of all kinds.

The ceremonies and sports linked with Holi are compared to those of the Portuguese Christmas. 'At the former the natives masquerade in every curious manner they can devise, and enact the part of wild beasts, and at the latter, after the manner of the ancient mysteries probably, the Portuguese dress up and act scenes.' Mrs Postans records in her journal (1838), that on such occasions of national mirth, the Hindu appeared 'in a natural and unaffected character. He gives licence to his general disposition, and laughs, sings and adorns himself with garlands, as if he still inherited his native soil, in a happy state of constitutional freedom.'

British observers were greatly impressed by the orderliness of these festive gatherings and processions. Sir John Malcolm in his *Memoirs of Central India* (1823) writes that Holi was the most popular with the lower classes. 'During the Carnival, which lasts four weeks, men forget both their restraints and distinctions, the poorest may cast the red powder upon his lord, the wife is freed from her habitual respect to her husband, and nothing but the song and dance is heard.'

Mountstewart Elphinstone, a scholar-cum-administrator (1840s), refers to the sports in which people eagerly joined during Holi and gives the following accounts of the festival:

> The boys dance round fires, sing licentious and satirical songs and give vent to all sorts of ribaldry against their superiors, by whom it is always taken in good part. The great sport of the occasion, however, consists in sprinkling each other with yellow liquid and throwing a crimson powder over each other's person. The liquid is also squirted through syringes and the powder is sometimes made up in large balls covered with icing-glass, which break as soon as they come in contact with the body. All ranks engage in this sport with enthusiasm and get into the spirit of the contest, till all parties are completely drenched with the red powder that they can scarcely be recognised. A great prime minister will invite a foreign ambassador to play the Holi at his house, and

will take his share in the most riotous parts of it with the ardour of a school boy.

According to Bishop Heber (1828), 'Holi is an occasion when drunkness is common among the Hindus!' In Gujarat, Forbes mentions in his *Oriental Memoirs* that a favourite diversion, very much similar to that on 1 April in England, was to 'send people on errands and expeditions that are to end in disappointment and raise a laugh at the expense of the person sent.'

Holi celebrations in the court of Scindia in Gwalior come alive in this fascinating account by Broughton (1809) who took part in the festivities there:

> When we visited Seendhiya to partake of this curious amusement, he received us in a tent, erected for the purpose . . . In front were assembled all the dancing girls in camp. We went dressed for the occasion in white linen jackets and pantaloons. The Maharaj himself began the amusements of the day by sprinkling a little red and yellow water upon us from *goolabdans,* which are small silver vessels kept for the purpose of sprinkling rose water at visitors. Everyone then began to throw about the *abeer* and squirt at his neighbours as he pleased. . . . we were alternately powdered and drenched till the floor on which we sat was covered some inches in depth with a kind of pink- and orange-coloured mud. Such a scene I never witnessed in my life.

Then Broughton describes the performance of the dancing girls:

> . . . bedecked with gold and silver lace, their tawdry trappings stained with patches of *abeer,* and dripping, like so many Naiads, with orange-coloured water, now chanting the Holi songs with all the airs of practised libertinism, and now shrinking with affected screams beneath a fresh shower from Maharaj.

He adds:

> The Holi songs are not necessarily indelicate. In the following one, Krishna, in his youthful character of *Kanaiha,* or the beloved, is described as attacked by a party of Gopees or maids, of Mathura during the time of Holi. As it portrays, with much accuracy and spirit, the peculiar customs of that festival, I have translated it:

> While some his loosen'd turban seize.
> And ask for Phag, and laughing tease;
> Others approach with roguish leer,
> And softly whisper in his ear.
> With many of scoff, and many of taunt,
> The Phagoon some fair Gopees chant;
> While others, as he bends his way,
> Sing at their doors Dhumaree gay.
> One boldly strikes a loving slap;
> And clouds of crimson dust arise
> About the youth with lotus-eyes.
> Then all the colour'd water pour.
> And whelm him in a saffron shower;
> And crowding round him bid him stand,
> With wands of flowers in every hand.

Broughton also describes the celebration of Holi by the ladies who assembled in tents or houses, had nautch parties all night and drenched one another with coloured water. No men, however, were admitted to these select parties except their husbands or sometimes their brothers of a tender age.

A somewhat similar account is given by Miss Fane, daughter of the British commander-in-chief who was invited to play Holi in 1837 by Maharaja Ranjit Singh at Lahore. Contemporary writings document the European attendance at Indian festivals. In the East India Company's army, the participation of British officers in the Holi was a matter of etiquette. The sepoys were delighted to see their British officers participate in their revelry and would often play practical jokes on unpopular officers.

Diwali held the pride of place in north India. Col. Todd, in his early-nineteenth-century classic, *Annals of Rajasthan*, traces the origin of this 'grand Oriental festival' to Central Asia. He writes that the Egyptians who furnished the Grecian pantheon, held these solemn festivals also called the feast of lamps in honour of Minerva at Lais and from there the Diwali radiated to remote China, the Nile, the Ganges and the shores of the Tigris. In this account of Diwali, one of the most brilliant fêtes of Rajasthan, Col. Todd states,

> . . . the Feast of Lamps is in honour of Lakshmi, the wife of Vishnu, the goddess of wealth, when every city, village and encampment exhibits a blaze of splendour. The potters' wheels revolve for weeks before solely for the manufacture of lamps (*diwa*) and from the palace to the peasant's hut, everyone supplies himself with them in proportion to his means, and arranges them according to his fancy. Stuffs, pieces of gold, and sweetmeats are carried in trays and consecrated at the temple of Lakshmi. On this day, it is incumbent on every votary of Lakshmi to try the chance of the dice, and from their success in the Diwali, the prince, the chief, the merchant and the artisan foretell the state of their coffers for the ensuing year.

The Rev. Ward in his *Religion of the Hindoos* (1817), however, admits that he cannot trace its origin.

> In the month of Kartik, the Hindoos suspend lamps in the air on bamboos in honour of the gods and in obedience to the *shastras*—as the offering of lamps to particular gods is considered as an act of merit, so this offering

to all the gods during the auspicious month of Kartik is supposed to procure many benefits to the giver.

Diwali on the ghats of Kanpur is made alive in a fascinating account (1830) by Fanny Parks.

> On reaching the ghat, I was quite delighted with the beauty of a scene resembling fairyland . . . On every temple, on every ghat, and on the steps down to the river's side, thousands of small lamps were placed from the foundation to the highest pinnacle, tracing the architecture in the lines of light. The evening was very dark, and the whole scene was reflected in the Ganges.

She describes how the crowds of Hindu worshippers prostrated themselves before the idols of Lord Shiva and Ganesha and then poured Ganges water, rice, oil and flowers over the images of the gods. She also noted some women sending off little paper boats, each containing a lamp, which floating down the river, added to the beauty of the scene. The river was covered with fleets of these little lamps hurried along by the rapid stream. She was so thrilled by the sight that she recorded:

> I was greatly pleased: so Eastern, so fairy-like a scene, I had not witnessed, since my arrival in India; nor could I have imagined that the dreary-looking station of Cawnpore contained so much of beauty.

It was not uncommon for the sahibs' houses to be illuminated on Diwali nights. The Godden sisters in their biographical work, *Two under the Indian Sun* (1966), offer a vivid account of Diwali celebrations in the early part of that century:

> We always kept Diwali in our home and all day, we helped or hindered Guru, Govind and all other gardeners

as they made the lamps ready and set them on die arch
verandah railing and window ledge. The Muslim servants
joined in the excitement for this was a festival enjoyed
by everyone; father told us that the Moghul Emperor
Akbar had illuminated his palace on this night.

Thrilled with their illuminated house they would go up
to the rooftop to catch a view of the bazaar, a ribbon
of brightness, and enjoy the sight as the little pointed
gold flames flickered and swayed gently, apparently of
their own accord, and at once shone steadily again.

Durga Puja, the biggest Hindu festival in Bengal,
finds repeated mention and there are several accounts
of lavish entertainment and festivities on this occasion.
Kali or Durga is described as the tutelary goddess of
Calcutta and Maria Graham (1811) records:

> On this occasion her images and those of some other
> divinities, were carried in procession with great pomp,
> and bathed in the Hoogly, which being a branch of the
> Ganges is sacred. The figures were placed under canopies,
> which were decked with the most gaudy colours, and
> carried upon men's heads. Several of these moving temples
> went together, preceded by musical instruments, banners,
> and bare-headed brahmins, repeating *muntras* (forms of
> prayer). The gods were followed by cars, drawn by oxen
> or horses gaily caparisoned, bearing the sacrificial utensils,
> accompanied by other Brahmins, and the procession
> was closed by an innumerable multitude of people of
> all castes. This feast lasted several days.

She also describes a fabulous nautch party organized by
Maharaja Rajkissen Bahadur who personally received
his guests, presented them with bouquets of flowers,
perfumed them with *ottur* and sprinkled rose water
on them. A number of contemporary accounts refer to

similar celebrations by the wealthy babus of Calcutta, some of whom succeeded in securing the presence of the Governor General, the commander-in-chief or other high dignitaries at these functions. Invitations were issued through letters and cards couched in a florid style as well as through advertisements in the local press.

Europeans attending Durga Puja (by Alexis Soltykoff, Calcutta, c. 1850)

An interesting announcement about the celebration of Durga Puja carried by the *Calcutta Gazette* of 9 November 1826 runs as follows:

> A native festival is to be celebrated at Baboo Rooploll Mullick's in the Chitpore Road on the evening of the 14th, 15th, and 16th instant, in the grandest and most splendid style, an English band will be in attendance, and the Nautches and Entertainments will excel every amusement of the kind ever witnessed at this Presidency.
>
> Tickets are under distribution to the Baboo's friends

and all the respectable Ladies and Gentlemen of the presidency, who may feel desirous of honouring the Baboo with their company.

Gunter and Hooper are to furnish the Supper, and to supply the best Champaign, Claret, and all kinds of wine and liquors, & c.

These accounts give an idea of the recreational aspect of religion in society at the time. But the lower classes or the outcasts of Hindu society tried to win the favour of gods through ritual self-mortification as depicted by the Charak Puja or the hook-swinging festival. Such rites of torture were prevalent in Bengal and some parts of south India. Fanny Parks in her eyewitness account (1820) describes this 'disgusting practice' of swinging by hooks. Upright poles were fixed in the ground, and at the top of each was another pole which revolved upon the first. The devotees were suspended to one end of the revolving pole by iron hooks stuck into their flesh, and were whirled round and round by a number of men. They carried bags in their hands from which they threw sweetmeats and flowers to the cheering crowds below. Some of them unable to endure the torture even died during the ordeal. There were other devotees who 'went about with small spears through their tongue and arms, and still more with hot irons pressed to their sides'.

Capt. Charles Gold, a distinguished amateur artist, describes hook-swinging as a barbarous ceremony. He witnessed it at Nagapattinam (1793) and made a sketch of a man hooked through the back and suspended in the air. The ceremony signified the homage paid by the pariah caste to Mariatale, the goddess of smallpox. He gives a detailed account and says that before hooking, the devotees were given strong intoxicants which made them almost insensible to pain and they regarded this dangerous ordeal as a pastime.

A young British cadet watching a nautch at Durga Puja celebrations (by Sir Charles D'Oyly, Calcutta, c. 1810)

The fairs were usually held once a year in most cities and villages. All kinds of shows and diverse entertainment were provided by the jugglers, acrobats, magicians, puppeteers, snake charmers, tamasha women and nautch girls. A truly glorious one was Kumbh Mela, the great fair at Hardwar on the banks of the Ganges, one of the important places of the Hindus for purification. In April the pilgrims flocked there not only from every part of India, but also from China, Persia and Bokhara. Every sixth and twelfth year, the concourse was so vast that at one festival there were more than two million present. Capt. Thomas Skinner who visited the Hardwar fair in the 1830s, wrote,

> . . . we had passed thousands of people on every description of vehicle hastening towards it. These were of

all ages, all costumes, and all complexions: no spot upon earth can produce so great a variety of the human race at one assemblage, and it will be impossible to enumerate the article of different sorts, or even the countries that produced them, offered for sale in the streets.

Emma Roberts in her account (1830) describes how troops of dancing girls had set up their camps at the fair and:

. . . were to be seen performing either in front of the houses of rich persons or in the interiors, all thrown open and lighted up every evening. The whole of the river, town and inhabited parts of the forest, presented a series of illuminations as soon as darkness commenced, this brilliant display being enlivened by occasional bursts of fireworks.

At some point of time Hardwar came to be better known for the Ardh Kumbh Mela, (held every sixth year), and the city of Allahabad, where the Ganges has a confluence (sangam) with the river Yamuna and the mythical river Saraswati, came to be recognized for the Kumbh Mela (held every twelfth year). These fairs continue to this day to be the meeting points of saints and sadhus of all descriptions, with ochre robes and some with no robes at all. They are worshipped by gullible men and women and decried by agnostics, the modern urban generation.

For Muslims, Muharram, a ten-day mourning for Husain, the son of Ali by Fatima, daughter of the Prophet, was one of the most important religious occasions. According to Dr E. Ives's account (1773):

. . . they carry about a model of the tomb of their ancestors, made of light bamboo and paper finely ornamented, for three days and nights, and are attended by people ridiculously dressed, shouting and dancing to the country music. On the last day of the festival, they carry these models into the fields with a kind of funeral procession, and there by breaking them in pieces put an end to the ceremony. One would also hear the discordant noises of drums, trumpets and matchlocks, mixed with the beating of breasts, loud sobbing and half-frantic exclamations of the devout Muslims.

Louis Rousellet (1860) describes how tazias, some measuring twenty feet in height, were carried through Bhopal by elephants in the grand procession. Enchanted by the concluding scene, he noted:

Night sets in, and thousands of torches with their red light add to the fantastic character of the scene. Above this shouting crowd, like one of those infernal sarabands imagined by Les Callot, one seems to see the high towers of the tazias suspended in the air like mystic temples, glittering with gold and tinsel and borne with grave and solemn step by the elephants, who look like living pedestals, half lost in the shade. The procession halts on the borders of the lake, and everything subsides into darkness and silence.

The festival of Id was marked with cheerful bustle and amusement when the princes offered camels in sacrifices. On the occasion of Id-ul-Fitr when the fasting month of Ramzan ended, there was rejoicing all around and the nawabs and chiefs led splendid processions to the mosques for prayers.

All accounts emphasize the fact that Muslims celebrated their festivals just like the Hindus, with the same earnestness and ostentation and amused themselves with dance and song and other entertainments, including feasts and sports.

The greatest festival for the British was Christmas, celebrated with more exuberance and splendour than at home. The glamour and glitter of the celebrations in 1780 were described in *Hicky's Bengal Gazette* as follows:

> Monday last being Christmas Day the morning was ushered in with firing of guns. A breakfast was given by the honourable Governor General at the Courthouse and at noon a most sumptuous dinner at which there were present many persons of Distinction. Several royal salutes were fired from the Grand battery at the Loll Diggy, everyone of which was wash'd down with Lumba Pillans of Loll Shrub and the evening concluded with a Ball, cheer'd and enlivened by the Grand illumination and excellent band of Music. The Ball was honoured with the company of many amiable British ladies, and the lustre of their natural beauty, outrivalled the brilliancy of their Diamonds and rendered them useless.

Writing on the same occasion, the Christmas of 1780, Eliza Fay informed her friends in England that 'keeping Christmas—though sinking into disuse at home—prevails here with all its ancient festivity'. She found that large plantain trees were placed on each side of the principal entrances and the gates and pillars were ornamented with wreaths of flowers, fancifully disposed, which beautified the scene. She also wrote about the public dinner at the government house and an 'elegant ball and supper' in the evening. These were repeated on the New Year's Day.

Another festive occasion for the sahibs was the celebration of the King's birthday that was observed with equal gaiety and grandeur. Again as reported in 1780, large guns were fired in the morning from the new forts accompanied by several volleys from smaller guns. The King's judges and other prominent ladies and gentlemen of the Calcutta Presidency were entertained by the Governor General and his wife with a grand party at the magnificent illuminated hall. The evening concluded with a ball with enchanting music by an excellent band.

21

Jugglers and Magicians

The most mind-boggling feats are said to have been performed by the professional jugglers of India. European accounts refer at length to their shows, including the famous rope trick, and other feats of legerdemain unknown in the West. Foreigners were so completely wonderstruck after seeing these that some of them attributed supernatural power to the jugglers. They were also amazed by extraordinary feats of manual dexterity displayed by acrobats and tumbling women. While complimenting them for their talents, some observers asked European performers to learn from their Indian counterparts whose feats were presented without the aid of elaborate appliances because they were skilled in the art of distracting the attention of observers at the critical moment.

The most controversial and mysterious of all is the legendary Indian rope trick which finds a mention in the Jatakas. In the eighth century, Shankaracharya speaks of 'the magician, the *mayavin*, who throws a cord up into the air, and armed, climbs up it, beyond the range of sight, to enter into battle and be dismembered; after his bodily parts have fallen to the ground, he is seen to rise up again and there is no concern over thinking about the reality of the magic trick that has been performed'.

A somewhat similar description of this miraculous feat is found in Sir Henry Yule's account of Marco Polo who had heard or seen it. The most popular version of this trick is, however, attributed to Ibn Batuta who witnessed it in Delhi in the fourteenth century. He wrote:

> The magician tossed a wooden ball, in which there were little holes threaded with long cords, into the air, high into the sky and out of sight. The conjurer then ordered an assistant to climb the cord; and he too passed out of the range of spectators' vision. Calling out the boy three times but not getting an answer, the magician himself in apparent anger, climbed the rope. Parts of the boy fell to earth—a hand, a foot, another hand, another foot, then the child's head, and finally the mutilated trunk. Descending, his robes stained with blood and gore, the magician made obeisance to the Khan and kissed the earth, and then much to the amazement and relief of a horrified Ibn Batuta, put the boy back together. Someone whispered, 'it's all just a magic trick.' The boy had not climbed the rope, the body had neither been dismembered nor reassembled and restored to life—it was like so many things we believe have taken place, all an illusion.

Then in the seventeenth century there is a graphic account of the rope trick in the memoirs of Jahangir who witnessed the performance at his court. By the end of the nineteenth century, newspapers in India and abroad carried reports by travellers who claimed to have witnessed the rope trick. The London-based *Morning Post,* at the turn of the twentieth century, carried the testimony of Sir Ralph Pearson, Lt governor of the North-West Frontier Province (NWFP), who had seen the rope trick in West Khandesh district of Bombay. In 1918 one Captain Holmes just back from India gave a lecture on the rope trick in London, complete with photographs of its performance at Kirkee near Poona.

Lord Fredrick Hamilton who thought he had seen the trick, theorized that it was the result of many salaams that the magician executed and produced a drugged audience and hallucinatory effects or mass hypnosis which helped the legend live. There were, however, many sceptics who dismissed it both as a miracle and as a trick. There were others who held that the legend tells a truth, that the trick was indeed performed, not just as a miracle but as an artful illusion. 'By directing his will, the magician causes his mental images to project themselves as real to the vision of his audience. In this way he produces an illusion—a force which the adepts call *Maya* whereby the senses of the observers report as fact things that have no real existence.'

Finally, the mystery of the trick is unravelled by A.C. Brown in his interesting book, *The Ordinary Man's India* (1927). He writes:

> The rope trick is more talked about than seen. But nevertheless there is a certain amount of truth in the story of this Eastern magic.

He cites the evidence of three Europeans, all of whom had actually seen the trick. The first is Lady Waghorn who had seen it near Madras in 1892 and wrote about it in the *Daily Mail*, testifying to the genuineness of the rope trick. She describes how standing about fifteen feet from the magician, she saw a fairly stout rope thrown up about twelve feet into the air. It became rigid, and a boy of about twelve climbed up and vanished at the top. A few minutes later he reappeared in the branches of a mango tree in the garden 100 yards away. The second testimony was given to the author by Mr Bodalin, a Dutchman living in Calcutta, who witnessed it on the maidan. His experience was similar to that described by Lady Waghorn, save only that after the boy had apparently ascended the rigid rope the magician himself ran up the rope and shouted to the boy to come down. There was no reply, so the magician in a rage whipped out a knife and slashed it wildly above his head. When he slid down the rope, the knife in his hand was dripping with what appeared to be blood. Soon thereafter, the boy appeared forcing his way to the centre from the outskirts of the crowd. Next, he relates the testimony of Colonel Barnard, commissioner of police in Calcutta, which really solves once and for all the mystery of the rope trick. The colonel was invited to attend a private performance of the rope trick in an Indian house. He asked another police officer to accompany him, and managed to take unobserved a small camera also. While the performance was going on the colonel managed to secure several snapshots of the proceedings. He saw the conjurer, the rope and the boy. He saw the rope thrown into the air; he saw it remain vertical and rigid. He saw the boy climb the rope and disappear into the air above. And a few moments later he saw the boy reappear, large as life, and stand again by the side of the conjurer. He was frankly amazed, and said so; but when he developed these negatives he found the camera had not seen as much as its master. There was the boy and the conjurer, but the rope was on the ground at the very moment when the colonel had seen it in the air. And the boy also was on the ground—shown clearly on each negative. The author concludes that as the camera cannot lie, its evidence had to be believed, so the only explanation possible is that the whole affair was an optical illusion. In other words, everybody knows what the rope trick is, they see what they expect and want to see, and are self-hypnotized.

Another popular show reported from the seventeenth century onwards was the mango trick. Here the juggler would plant a mango stone in the ground and show at brief intervals the plant rising above the ground and successively producing leaves, flowers and fruit as he continued with his incantations. Both Tavernier and Bernier have given descriptions of this trick. So also the Rev. Ovington (1688) who believed that it was due to black magic, because a gentleman became ill after eating one of the mangoes and did not recover until he followed a brahmin's advice; he restored it to the juggler. An English chaplain on seeing the trick protested against Christians witnessing such shows which involved the display of non-Christian powers.

There are several descriptions of the mango trick which are more or less repetitive, but we come across an interesting account of a female juggler at Madras who had in her own house frequently converted a stone into a mango tree.

Taking a plain round pebble from the seashore, it was placed by her in an earthenware dish filled with earth, which was then watered and covered by a cloth. Spirits by whose aid such wonders can be brought were then invoked; the cloth was lifted and a tiny green plant was seen just emerging from the ground. The plant was again watered, again covered and the spirits were invoked anew. On the cloth being removed a second time, the little tree was found to be grown and well stocked with bright coloured mangoes—the whole process occupying only a quarter of an hour.

The mango trick, according to Dr Francis Buchanan (1814) was one of the stock tricks of the Indian juggler and could be seen any day in Canara, Mysore and Malabar.

Another trick, considered an unprecedented one in the annals of jugglery by Europeans, was the basket trick involving the mysterious disappearance of a girl. It was an instance of visual illusion and appeared to contain an element of the marvellous. The Rev. Caunter in his journal (1834) gives a vivid description of this trick:

. . . stout, ferocious-looking fellow stepped forward with a common wicker basket of the country, which he begged we would carefully examine. This we accordingly did; it was the slightest texture and admitted the light through a thousand apertures. Under this fragile covering he placed a child about eight years old, an interesting little girl, habited in the only garb which nature had provided for her, perfect frame and elastic of limb—a model for a cherub and scarcely darker than a child of southern France. When she was properly secured, the man, with a lowering aspect, asked her some questions, which she instantly answered; and as the thing was done within a few feet from the spot on which we were seated, the voice appeared to come so distinctly from the basket, that I felt at once satisfied there was no deception. They held a conversation for some moments, when the juggler, almost with a scream of passion, threatened to kill her. There was a stern reality in the whole scene which was perfectly dismaying; it was acted to the life, but terrible to see and hear. The child was heard to beg for mercy, when the man seized a sword, placed his foot upon the frail wicker covering under which his supposed victim was so piteously supplicating his forbearance and, to my absolute consternation and horror, plunged it through, withdrawing it several times and repeating the plunge with all the blind ferocity of an excited demon. By this time his countenance exhibited an expression fearfully indicative of the most frantic of human passions. The shrieks of the child were so real and distracting, that they almost curdled for a moment the whole mass of my blood: my first impulse was to rush upon the monster and fell him to the earth; but he was armed and I defenceless. I looked at my companions—they appeared to be pale and paralysed with terror; and yet these feelings were somewhat neutralized by the consciousness that the man could not dare to commit a deliberate murder in the broad eye of day, and before so many witnesses; still the whole thing was appalling. The blood ran in streams from the basket; the child was heard to struggle under it; her groans fell horridly upon the ear; her struggles smote painfully upon the heart. The former were gradually subdued into a faint moan and the latter into a slight rustling sound; we seemed to hear the last convulsive gasp which was to set her innocent soul free from the gored body, when to our inexpressible astonishment and relief, after muttering a few cabalistic words, the juggler took up the basket, but no child was to be seen. The spot was indeed dyed with blood but there were no mortal remains, and after a few moments of undissembled wonder, we perceived the little object of our alarm coming towards us among the crowd. She advanced and saluted us, holding out her hand for our donations, which we bestowed with hearty goodwill; she received them with a most graceful salaam and the party left us, well satisfied with our more than expected gratuity. What rendered the deception the more extraordinary was that the man stood aloof from the crowd during the whole performance—there was not a person within several feet of him.

The French traveller, Louis Rousselet (1860s), who also witnessed the basket trick noted that it was one of the most curious tricks of the East.

Another amazing feat which bewildered spectators was the swallowing of a sword blade apparently at the risk of one's life. It is described at great length by James Forbes in his *Oriental Memoirs* (1813).

> Seating himself the juggler took the sword, which had a straight blade, about 26 inches in length and one in breadth, with edges and point blunted, and after oiling it, he introduced the point into his mouth and pushed it gently down his throat.

He pushed it until the hand of Forbes, who held the hilt, came in contact with his lips. 'He then made a sign to me,' says the writer, 'with one of his hands, to feel the point of sword between his breast and navel, which I could plainly do by bending him a little more backwards, and pressing my fingers on his stomach.' On withdrawing the blade, blood was seen on some parts of it.

Sir Thomas Munro in his narrative (c.1810) mentions that the juggler, after showing his skill with the sword blade, swallowed a complete horse's tail about two feet long, introducing it into his mouth by the lower end, and gorging it to the very stump, without distorting a feature in his face, though the uneven hairs must have pricked his throat as they descended. Dr Fryer saw a juggler (c.1700) who swallowed a chain and made it clink in his stomach, while F. Wyman (c.1860) saw one swallowing baskets full of knives, nails and tape. Lucknow used to boast of its special swallowers who could gulp a billiard ball or half a dozen birds and reproduce them on demand.

Henry Grose in his journal (1750–64) gives an astonishing story of the jugglers and pays high tributes to their humane approach and compassion:

A long boat with men going from an English ship, to Calcutta, a fortified settlement we have on the banks of the Ganges, in Bengal, stopped short of it a considerable way, waiting for the return of the tide, and went on shore to a Moorish village, where just at that time were some of the jugglers showing to a mob gathered round them their various tricks; one of which, and no juggle, was the firing of a pistol loaded with powder down one of their throats. On the arrival of the sailors, this was to be repeated, for they had before done it; but their powder having been consumed, one of the sailors offered the man

Juggler swallowing a sword blade (by Captain Charles Gold, c. 1790)

some he had about him. It was accepted and the effect
of it was that being much stronger than what they used
for this purpose, it killed the man upon the spot. As he
was a Mahomedan, and the whole village was so, the
mob instantly rose, and were preparing to massacre all
the sailors there, in revenge for the Mussulman's blood
and would infallibly have done so, but for the humane
interposition of the jugglers themselves, who declared,
that however sorry they might be for the death of their
brother, it was no means imputable to the English, who
were evidently clear of any malicious design in it. This
alone appeased the populace and the sailors were suffered
to return quietly to their boat.

Levitation shows have also been recorded by many
travellers. According to Thomas Frost:

> . . . the serial suspension was performed in 1820s
> at Madras by an old Brahmin Seshal, with no better
> apparatus than a piece of plank, which with four legs,
> he formed into an oblong stool; and upon which, in a
> little brass socket, he placed in a perpendicular position,
> a hollow bamboo, from which projected a kind of crutch,
> covered with a piece of common hide— he was seen poised
> in the air about four feet from the ground in a sitting
> attitude, the outer end of one hand merely touching the
> crutch, with fingers deliberately counting beads, and the
> other hand and arm held up in an erect posture.

In 1875, Harry Keller, in the company of the Prince of
Wales witnessed a levitation in the maidan of Calcutta.
It was believed that some Indian yogis, through spiritual
means, could defy physical laws.

Among other clever tricks, there are descriptions of
jugglers changing pebbles into birds, birds into eggs and
eggs into plants; they would thread beads with their
tongues, join innumerable pieces of cotton into one long
cord, keep half a score of sharp knives in the air at once,

throw cannon balls with their toes, spin tops on the ends of twigs and make rings and coins move about on the ground with a kind of dancing or jerking motion. One of the favourite tricks was to borrow a watch and transport it to some unthought-of place and send the owner to find it. There are authentic accounts of all these tricks by those who had witnessed these shows.

In 1814, a party of Indian jugglers consisting of two men and a boy were taken to England from Madras by the captain of the *Monarch*. They demonstrated their art at Pall Mall three times a day and created a sensation. They jolted the English artistes who could only manage leaping and rope dancing.

As regards feats of manual skill, Indians were considered unequalled in the world. Their physical

Man levitating (by Johan Gantz, c. 1820)

strength too was perfectly amazing considering their simple diet and the climate in which they lived. Among their extraordinary feats may be mentioned somersaults and capers made with wonderful agility, crossing elephants and camels, jumping through a frame supporting a dozen cut glasses and many other arduous exercises requiring extreme caution and delicacy. The skill and strength displayed by women was equally dazzling. Dr Fryer saw a woman who held nine gilded balls in play with her hands and feet and the muscles of the arms and legs, for a long time together without letting them fall. J.D. Gay, special correspondent of the *Daily Telegraph* who accompanied the Prince of Wales in 1875, speaks about a stout girl who threw a man weighing 11 stones over her shoulders, then seizing him once more, placing him crossways on her back and tossing him into the air as though he were made of feathers and not a broad-shouldered human being. Turning backwards on her feet she picked up straws with her eyelids, threw somersaults and lifted weights which would have astonished any London acrobat. There were also little girls rolling themselves into balls, tying themselves into knots, going through a bewildering amount of dislocation, and with their eyes bandaged, threading a needle with their toes.

According to the Rev. Caunter (1830s) the most extraordinary feat performed by a woman was the egg dance, an act of 'manual dexterity' never witnessed anywhere else in the world. He describes it as follows:

> A woman, young and beautifully formed, fixed on her head a fillet of a stiff, strong texture, to which were fastened, at equal distances, twenty pieces of string of equal lengths, with a common noose at the end of each.

Under her arm she carried a basket, in which twenty
fowl's eggs were carefully deposited. Her basket, the fillet,
and the nooses, were severally examined by companions
and myself—there was evidently no deception. It
was broad daylight, the basket was of the simplest
construction, the eggs and strings were all manifestly
what they were represented to be; nor, in fact, had the
woman anything about her to aid deception, had she
been disposed to practise it. She advanced alone and
stood before us, within a few feet of where we were
seated. She then began to move rapidly round upon a
spot not more than eighteen inches in diameter, from
which she never for an instant deviated, though, after a
few moments, her rotation had become so exceedingly
rapid as to render it all but painful to look at her. She
absolutely spun round like a top.

When her body had reached its extreme point of
acceleration, she quietly drew down one of the strings
which had formed a horizontal circle round her and
put an egg into the noose; when this secured, she
jerked it back to its original position, still continuing
her gyrations with undiminished velocity and repeating
the process until she had secured the whole twenty eggs
in the nooses previously prepared to receive them. She
projected them rapidly from her hand the moment she
had secured them, until at length the whole were flying
round her in one unbroken circular line. After the eggs
had been thus slung, she continued her motion for full five
minutes, without the least diminution of her velocity, to
our undissembled astonishment; when, taking the strings
one by one, she displaced the eggs from their respective
nooses, laid them in her basket, and then in one instant
stopped, without the movement of a limb, or even the
vibration of a muscle, as if she had been suddenly fixed
into marble. Her countenance was perfectly calm; she
exhibited not the slightest distress from her extraordinary
exertions, but received our applauses with an apparent
modesty of demeanour.

Among other street performers were the bazigars or acrobats who performed stunts such as dancing on long stilts, climbing and balancing poles. A real delight for European children was the kutpootliwallah or the puppet player. The comedy played by him was mainly a procession of rajas who entered two and two in a durbar but there was an undercurrent of farce which gave some life to the exhibition. There would be a comic scene of wayfarer robbed by a thief and bullied by a policeman, a satirical character. The sahibs engaged them to present special shows for the amusement of their children.

Finally, there was the common bunderwallah who roamed about the town with three or four monkeys and a goat. He made them dance to the beat of his hand drum and performed several wonderful tricks with the goat which also served as a mount for the monkeys. The monkeys also performed many laughable tricks at the bidding of the bunderwallah.

It is a pity that many of the skills of Indian jugglers and other street performers have long disappeared from the Indian scene. As is well known, the Indian art of jugglery from time immemorial was handed down from father to son and it was always a well-guarded secret in a family. In the course of time, performers died without imparting the secret of their art to anyone. But for the detailed accounts left behind by foreign visitors and sketches by the European artists, we would have remained ignorant about some of the wonderful feats of our performing artistes in this field.

22

Caste and Social Order

Foreigners were surprised to discover that Indian society was divided into social classes on the basis of birth. The institution of the Hindu caste system, as Max Weber observed, 'signified the enhancement and transformation of social distance into a religion'. Dominated by the Hindu environment, the Muslims could not escape the influence of caste, and different classes adopted social grades for people according to birth. The arithmetic of caste played a dominant part in determining the vocational pursuits of people. Even the British society in India could not remain immune to its influence and erected class distinctions of their own, undreamt of at home.

'Mankind has a passion for classifying itself,' wrote Lord Meston,

> and ever since the days of Plato and Herodotus, ancient societies have been described as being divided into classes which had no intermarriage or community of interest. It was left to India to develop this ancient idea into a system of incredible complexity. It survives in full force

today, when in all other civilised countries, the theory
has faded into a tradition.

No other people have erected a social structure
comparable to the caste system of India. The origin of
the system has been much debated but it is believed that
the great lawgiver Manu defined the laws of castes to
be incorporated into a system of Hindu law.

The word caste is derived from the Portuguese word
casta meaning purity of breed. It was used by the early
Portuguese settlers in India. The ancient Indian word for
caste was varna. According to Hindu belief, the supreme
god Brahma, the Lord of Creation, caused the brahmin
to spring from his mouth, the kshatriya from his arms,
the vaishya from his thighs and the shudra from his
feet. To each one of them, the lord assigned separate
duties and occupations. The brahmins were required
to teach and study the scriptures. He commanded the
kshatriya to protect the people, the vaishya to till the
land, tend cattle and engage in commerce, and ordered
the shudra to serve the other three castes. Everyone
believed that the whole structure of Hindu life had the
sanction of gods.

In Indian society, the Hindu was always known by
his caste—'a man without caste was an insulting epithet
which in no case could be forgiven or forgotten.' The
Hindu's attachment to caste, both high and low, was
so forceful that it proved to be one of the chief hurdles
for Christian missionaries to convert them. Referring to
the pride of caste, H.H. Wilson (1861) says:

> The lowest native is no outcaste, he has an acknowledged
> place in society, he is the member of a class; and he is
> invariably more retentive of the distinction than those
> above him. In depicting the horrors of the system,

European writers lose sight of the compensations. The veriest *chandala* who is one of a community is less miserable, less unhappy, than many of the paupers of the civilised communities of Europe, with whom no man owns companionship or kindred. They are the true outcastes, not the Pariah or Chandala.

Abbe Dubois counters criticism of the Hindu caste system and highlights its advantages:

I believe caste division to be in many respects the *chef d'oeuvre,* the happiest effort, of Hindu legislation. I am persuaded that it is simply and solely due to the distribution of people into castes, that India did not lapse into a state of barbarism, and that she preserved and perfected the arts and sciences of civilisation whilst most other nations of the earth remained in a state of barbarism. I do not consider caste to be free from many great drawbacks, but I believe the resulting advantages, in the case of a nation constituted like the Hindus more than outweigh the resulting evils . . .

Caste assigns to each individual his own profession or calling and the handing down of this system from father to son from generation to generation, makes it impossible for any person or his descendents to change the conditions of life which the law assigns to him for any other. Such institution was probably the only means that the most clear-sighted prudence could devise for maintaining a state of civilization amongst a people endowed with the peculiar characteristics of the Hindus.

Social sanction for a profession or calling was based on the sheer accident of birth. According to Sir Charles D'Oyly, prejudices pertaining to professions were also wedded to social distinctions of castes. Few would normally accept work which lowered the traditional repute and dignity of their caste. This was the reason why the English residents had to employ an army of servants for different kinds of duties in their households.

Caste governed the code of conduct, religious rituals and practice and even food habits and clothing. The different classes were barred from free intercourse with each other, 'the inferior ones were necessarily excluded from intimate social contacts with the superiors'. Intercaste marriages were beyond the comprehension of people for fear of excommunication from society. Even inter-dining with lower castes was ruled out. Indian women lost their caste when they married Europeans or established a liaison with them. Their progeny were called half-castes or Eurasians and later Anglo-Indians, who were disowned by Indian society. In order to defend its honour, caste exercised close control over its members. Every caste had its own customs and traditions and those deviating from them were duly punished. 'Permanent exclusion from caste was the severest penalty that the caste could pass against any of its members. Once a family was thus socially degraded, nothing could materially restore it to its pristine position.' Incidentally, many a victim of this harsh treatment was welcomed by missionaries into their flock.

The Hindus not only divided society into four groups but also divided an individual's life into four stages (ashrams). The first stage called brahmacharya, a span of twenty-five years, was to be devoted to studies and learning, followed by grihastha, a similar span of life as a householder, raising a family and working for material progress. The third stage, vanaprastha, involved public service without profit, and finally the last stage, sanyasa, demanded total detachment from worldly activities and a life of a recluse preparing for the ultimate merging with the divine.

Muslim society, though not strictly divided like the Hindu castes, adopted a scheme of social gradation based on birth. Contemporary writings refer to two main social divisions, Sharaf or the high-born, and Razil, the low-born. The former constituted the gentry or classes which claimed high extraction and could be compared to the brahmins and kshatriyas of the Hindu society. The latter group included menial workers and those engaged in lower professions like barbers, butchers and potters. Henry Martyn (1837) points out that the democratic ideals of Islam had been successfully challenged and undermined by the reactionary influences of caste. The Muslim classes that were of Hindu stock retained caste in full vigour. Further, class distinction, on the basis of ancestry or places of origin, was strongly supported, and accordingly Sheikhs, Mughals, Pathans and Persians were distributed into many small classes.

By the beginning of the nineteenth century, the growing power and prestige of the British brought about several changes in the Indian economic scene. The vested interests established by castes started disintegrating and the spectre of poverty and starvation often compelled some high-caste Hindus to humble themselves by lower professions. At the same time, some lower castes intruded into superior professions. About Bengal, H.T. Colebrooke (1807) wrote that 'every profession with few exceptions is open to every description of persons and the discouragement arising from religious prejudices is not greater than what exists in Great Britain from the effects of municipal and corporation laws.' The overall impact of these developments on the institution of caste system was, however, quite marginal and the entire Indian social structure continued to be dominated by the caste system which was the basis for social stratification not only among the Hindus but also among the Muslims.

It is interesting to observe how the British community in India came under the influence of caste system and evolved a peculiar snobbery of its own and created distinctions among its members. They developed a class system that was far more brutal than the one they had left behind. This system of social stratification has often been compared to the more rigid Indian caste system which the British found objectionable and frequently blamed for social problems and race relations in particular. Following this analogy the brahmins were the government civilian officials, followed by army officers, the warriors or kshatriyas. The merchants constituted the vaishyas group called box-wallahs who were socially kept at a distance by the former. The last in the social strata were the ordinary soldiers, tailors, barbers, half-castes or Eurasians corresponding to the shudras.

A satirical ballad of 1852 aptly illustrates the caste system of the British society in India:

On the banks of Ganges' water
When the wind blew fierce and hot,
Was the planter's lovely daughter,
Fairest of the lot;
For his bride a soldier sought her,
But Pa and Ma said nay,
And the planter's lovely daughter
Might not disobey.

On the banks of Ganges' water,
When the rainy season fell,
There I saw the planter's daughter.
All called her the belle;
Now another lover sought her,

A rich civilian he,
On the banks of Ganges' water,
None so sad as she.

On the banks of Ganges' water,
When the pleasant winter came,
Still was seen the planter's daughter,
And her soldier flame;
But the planter's lovely daughter
From thoughts of him were free,
On the banks of Ganges' water,
A judge's bride was she.

23

Thugs and Robbers

For centuries, thugs, members of a secret murderous society, were a menace to travellers in India. They believed that it was their divine mission to lure and kill fellow men. Booty was their right, if not reward. It was General Sleeman under the administration of Lord William Bentinck who enforced the strong arm of British law and stamped out this evil.

The word 'thug' is presumably derived from the Sanskrit word *thugna* (to deceive). The origin of thugs may be traced back to the Mughal times. During the reign of Akbar, no less than 500 thugs were executed in Itawah province. According to the French traveller Thevenot (1630s) the road between Delhi and Agra was full of thugs, 'the cunningest robbers all over the world'. They were not ordinary criminals who murdered simply for monetary gain; their ritual murders and methods were supposed to have religious sanction. According to legend, a great demon infested the earth devouring people. To save mankind, the goddess Kali attacked the demon and cut him down; but from his blood other demons rose. The goddess then created two men whom she gave handkerchiefs and taught them to strangle the demons without shedding their blood. All the demons were then destroyed. Thereafter she ordered them to keep the handkerchiefs as a remembrance and use them as weapons to continue killing, generation to generation, and earn a good living too.

The thugs claimed to enjoy the protection of the goddess Kali. The profession of thugee became hereditary. Thugs recruited members of gangs from all castes and classes, including Muslims. An interesting aspect of thugee was its ability to bind Hindus and Muslims together under the canopy of crime. The thugs of both groups worshipped Kali in the Hindu way.

The British authorities knew little about the existence of thugs as a body of dangerous criminals operating all over India, united by a secret code of conduct, until a whole band was captured near Bangalore after the storming of Seringapatnam (1799). Later in 1810, a number of sepoys disappeared during their journey home on leave. This was followed by the murder of a British lieutenant. An attack was launched on the villages where the assassins were known to live. Thus the widespread and vile crimes of these murderous gangs were exposed.

Young recruits were initiated to become thugs after rituals and ceremonies. A beginner was given a 'sacred' pickaxe, the symbol of the sect, and taught its secret language and signs. He took vows in the name of the goddess Kali to kill every human being who fell into his power. Then he took the 'holy food', a bit of coarse sugar, while other members sought blessings of the goddess. He was given a stern warning never to break his oath as otherwise he would face a horrible death as punishment by the great goddess. Transformed into a thug, he was allowed to try his 'prentice hand' on the throat of some sleeping traveller. A roomal, or handkerchief, properly noosed, was given by the guru or priest to the assassin and in return he received the coin taken from the pocket of the first victim. The pickaxe consecrated with many ceremonies, was used to dig a grave to bury the victims.

Before going on their adventures, the thugs would sacrifice a goat to propitiate goddess Kali. They never moved out without ascertaining good omens communicated to them by the goddess through animals and birds. The donkey held the pride of place and was considered 'equal to a hundred birds' and its braying was taken as an auspicious sign for their success. The next was the jackal and if it crossed the path from right to left it was an indication that a booty of gold lay ahead of the thugs. The deer, wolf and birds were also signals. To hear a crow cawing in flight was a bad omen which made them give up their expedition.

Thugs and their wicked operations were surrounded by mystery, created partly by their oath of secrecy and partly by a sham of respectable living usually as craftsmen in villages. They operated in areas far away from their homes so as not to be detected. Contemporary records describe their modus operandi:

> They waited at the caravanserais, or loitered about the roads in quest of travellers. Emissaries were employed to collect information on their movements; children and even handsome women were initiated into their horrid practices, the objective being to gain the confidence of the unwary to join their party, and then a favourable opportunity was taken to murder them. All of a sudden, a strip of cloth or an unfolded turban, was thrown round the neck of the unsuspecting stranger, and tightened till he was suffocated. Everyone of his companions would be murdered in the same way, and the bodies, after being

plundered, were carefully buried. Possessing the most ample means for gaining extensive information, they contrived to murder, in general only those who were not likely to be inquired for or soon missed, and whose disappearance might be accounted for by voluntary flight. Thus, a poor soldier was a safe victim, as absence from his regiment would be attributed to desertion. A servant entrusted with money was another, the conclusion being, when no trace was found of him, that he had betrayed his trust and run away . . .

After death was complete, the sacred pickaxe was called into play. A hole, about three feet deep, received the unfortunate, who was then buried with his face downwards, his corpse being first mangled to expedite decomposition and prevent its inflation, which by causing fissures in the earth might attract wild animals and reveal the body. If haste or alarm did not permit internment, it was flung into the nearest well or tank. An effusion of blood was avoided, and an impenetrable veil of darkness was thrown over all their atrocities. During

Thugs in the prison of Aurangabad from *India and its Native Princes* (by Louis Rousselet, c. 1880)

the attack, every possible precaution was taken to guard
against surprise; scouts were placed in every direction,
and should any one approach without being previously
seen, the nearest of these would throw himself on the
ground in a pretended fit and thus attract attention till
the body was concealed. If this failed, it was covered
with a cloth and the murderers feigned to be lamenting
the death of a friend. They have been known to travel
for days with the person they proposed to murder, till
a sufficiently favourable opportunity occurred.

Following their prescribed code, thugs did not attack
certain classes and individuals. Women were usually
spared in deference to goddess Kali. Holy men, poets,
musicians, certain craftsmen, and carriers of Ganges water
enjoyed their protection. Afraid of reprisals from colonial
rulers they refrained from attacking Europeans.

There was another branch of thugs who plied their
murderous trade on the main rivers. They became
boatmen, and invited travellers to take a boat ride on
payment. Then in midstream they would attack them
and throw their bodies into the river.

Determined to stamp out this evil, Lord William
Bentinck set up a special department to investigate and
destroy the thug and William Sleeman was placed in
charge of the whole operation in 1835. He organized
a body of sepoys as detective police and arrests were
then made while others were induced to turn approvers.
He launched a ruthless drive and the network of this
murderous gang was unearthed. Whereas earlier there
had been a sense of mystery about the thugs, Sleeman
claimed that all secrets of this murderous guild had
been exposed. 'I am satisfied', he wrote, 'that there is
no term, no rite, no ceremony, no omen or usage that
they have intentionally concealed from me.'

By 1837 more than 3,000 thugs were captured. Some of them were hanged, others transported, and the remaining were sent to prison.

Dacoity was another form of crime and dacoits also formed an organized fraternity. They belonged to certain castes and claimed pillage to be their hereditary calling. They targetted the wealthy or even a whole village for booty. They plundered with such speed and efficiency that resistance was seldom possible. They would smear their naked bodies with oil so that it was impossible to hold them. *Hicky's Gazette* recommended that a long bamboo with a triple iron hook at the end of it be kept in readiness to catch and detain such unwanted visitors.

Dacoits did not spare Europeans. Noted for their agility they would enter a bungalow by breaking through a wall and remove everything worth taking, leaving the owners, without waking them, in their night clothes. When approaching tents, they would imitate the howling of a dog or cries of a jackal and crawl on their bellies, making a small incision at the bottom of the tent. Many robberies were committed in this fashion and even the tent of the governor of Madras near Trichinopoly was not spared. The thieves took away all its contents including His Excellency's wearing apparel.

In 1795, a gang of five Europeans and a native were caught committing a burglary in the house of a rich native. This gang, having committed various burglaries, was a formidable set of thieves. Burglary at that time was a capital crime and all of them were hanged. Under the pressure of British law and exemplary punishment, the widespread evil of dacoity and robbery was also suppressed to a great extent.

24

Banning of an Indian Erotic Epic

Apsaras, the divine courtesans who adorned the court of Indra, lord of the firmament, entertained the gods by dancing merrily to the accompaniment of music by gandharvas. Urvashi, peer among the apsaras is said to have been born on earth as a devadasi who imparted divine knowledge of dance and music to human beings.

The institution of devadasis existed all over India. The Chinese pilgrim Hiuen Tsang, who visited India in the seventh century, testified to the existence of a well-established institution of temple dancers. However, after the advent of Muslim rule, devadasis disappeared from north India but the practice continued in the south until the beginning of the twentieth century.

Under the generous patronage of the Pallava, Chola, Pandya, and Nayaka kings, devadasis were honoured with titles and gifts in their heyday in the south, and their names are even mentioned in temple chronicles and inscriptions. They were trained from childhood in the arts of dance and music and were also taught classical literature in Sanskrit, Tamil, and Telugu.

222

Devadasis from Andhra Pradesh dominated the cultural scene in south India. The celebrated courtesan Muddupalani adorned the royal court of the Nayaka king of Tanjore, Partapsimha (1739–63), who was a great patron and lover of music, literature, and the arts. He honoured and rewarded Muddupalani not only for her accomplishments in the performing arts but also for her scholarly achievements as a learned poet well versed in Telugu and Sanskrit. At that time, the Tanjore court was one of the few surviving Hindu patrons of the arts in India and attracted the best talent from other parts of the country.

Muddupalani's marvellous erotic epic *Radhika Santwanam* (Appeasing Radha) is a mid-eighteenth-century literary masterpiece and a gem of Telugu literature. But it was little known outside Andhra Pradesh. Credit goes to Susie Tharu and K. Lalita for bringing to light this great work through their compilation, *Women Writing in India—600 BC to the Present*, published in the early 1990s. *Radhika Santwanam* consists of five hundred and eighty-four poems presenting the story of Radha and Krishna in a new light, and is replete with *shringara rasa* or erotic imagery. It describes the story of Radha who brings up Ila Devi from childhood and then gives her in marriage to Krishna. There is a graphic account of Radha's detailed instructions to the young bride on the technique of love-making and the art of responding to Krishna's foreplay and motions. Then Radha, overtaken by grief at the separation from Krishna, taunts him in anger for neglecting her, as she is herself deeply attached to him.

Krishna then appeases her with his divine loving embraces—Muddupalani's classic poem takes its title from this episode. Later, there is an amusing narration of Radha's aggressive role and initiative in making love to Krishna when he is not in the mood. Muddupalani is unconventional in her perception and treatment of the subject. She highlights a woman's initiative in love, and the woman's gratification forms the central theme of this literary work. There is also an absorbing account of a young girl's coming of age and her maiden sexual experience. She finds faults with men for being unstable, impetuous, and unreliable.

Perhaps Muddupalani was inspired to write this book on the basis of her professional experience with men who sought her favours for love and romance. This erotic epic became so controversial that it attracted even the government's notice and censorship on moral grounds.

Hailing from a family of devadasis, Muddupalani speaks with pride about the literary achievements of her mother and grandmother who were both poets. In her autobiographical prologue, she proclaims her own eminence and popularity as a poet and scholar. She also describes with confidence and pride her physical beauty and charm, her gracious personality and her generous patronage of young artists and writers. She introduces herself with the following verse:

> Which other woman of my kind has
> felicitated scholars with gifts of money?
> To which other woman of kind have
> epics been dedicated?
> Which other woman of my kind has
> won such acclaim in each of the arts?
> You are incomparable,
> Muddupalani among your kind.

The first version of *Radhika Santwanam* was published in 1887 and a second edition with a commentary by Venkatanarsu, an associate of the orientalist lexicographer

C.P. Brown, was brought out in 1907. This, however, omitted couplets of several poems as also Muddupalani's autobiographical prologue which tells readers about her accomplishments and eminence as a poet in the royal court. It was in 1910 that Nagaratnamma, a patron of the arts and a learned devadasi from Bangalore, not satisfied with the published version, decided to bring out the classic work in its original form. After extensive research, she finally succeeded in tracing the original palm-leaf manuscript of this work and she published the new edition in 1910. Speaking about her determination to bring this masterpiece to the attention of the intelligentsia and general readers, she wrote in the preface that she could not resist the temptation of reading this book over and over again. She also highlights the fact that this epic brimming with rasa was not only written by a woman, but also by one born into her own community.

The following verse from *Radhika Santwanam* reveals Muddupalani's mastery of portraying visual images invoking the basic emotions of joy, excitement, sensual pleasure, and sexual bliss:

Move on her lips
the tip of your tongue;
do not scare her
by biting hard,
place on her cheeks
a gentle kiss;
do not scratch her
with your sharp nails.
Hold her nipple
with your fingertips;
do not scare her
by squeezing it tight.
Make love
gradually;

do not scare her
by being aggressive
I am a fool
to tell you all these.
When you meet her
and wage your war of love
would you care of recall
my 'do's and dont's', honey?

—Translated by B.V.L. Narayanarow

(*Women Writing in India* edited by Susie Tharu and K. Lalita)

The above verse clearly shows that Muddupalani was an erudite scholar of Sanskrit literature and conversant with the writings of shringara rasa poets like Bhartrihari, Dandin, and Bilhana.

The publication of Muddupalani's classic work aroused lot of controversy and outright condemnation by contemporary social reformers. Many of them denounced it as obscene and labelled Muddupalani a fallen woman.

A leading social reformer of Madras wrote, 'many parts of the book are such that they should never be heard by a woman, let alone emerge from a woman's mouth. Using *shringar rasa* as an excuse Muddupalani shamelessly fills her poem with crude descriptions of sex.'

This was also the time when the anti-nautch campaign was in full swing in south India. Western-educated Indian reformers were alienated from the art and cultural traditions of the country and were influenced by the writings of the Madras Christian Literacy Society, which condemned devadasis in extremely harsh terms. The reformers even solicited for the anti-nautch movement the support of the governor of Madras and the viceroy. This moral censorship dealt a death blow to the traditional arts of dance and music and the devadasi institution.

As part of an imperial design to justify their rule as a civilizing mission, Indian cultural and traditional arts and customs were condemned as irrational and perverse. Not surprisingly, when the government translator presented the English version of parts of *Radhika Santwanam* to the authorities, the government, already under pressure from the reformers, decided that the book would endanger the moral health of their Indian subjects and banned it. Nagaratnamma gave a strong rejoinder to every criticism and put up a spirited defence but to no avail. There was a strong protest by the publishers who questioned the application of the Indian Penal Code 'to ancient classics that have been in circulation for centuries'. A conference of learned scholars also considered government interference in this field as 'inexpedient and undesirable and highly detrimental to the preservation and progress of Telugu literature'. But the government stuck to its decision and in 1911 all copies of the book were seized by the police and destroyed. Nagaratnamma's publishers were charged with producing an obscene book.

It was only after Independence in 1947 that the ban was withdrawn. The chief minister of Madras, T. Prakasan, remarked, 'it had been a battle for pearls of great beauty to be replaced in the necklace of Telugu literature'. The publishers were also given permission to republish Nagaratnamma's edition *of Radhika Santwanam*, which was released again in 1952. What a boon it would be for lovers of literature not only in India but also abroad if this book is translated into English and other Indian languages.

25

Splendid Sahibs

The early settlers were generally very influenced by Indian lifestyle and culture. Unaffected by racial prejudice, which was yet to show its ugly appearance, sahibs mixed freely with Indians on equal terms. It is only after India became a part of the Queen's Empire that the Englishmen, living in their islands of cantonments and civil stations, became aloof. As British power was on the rise in the eighteenth and early nineteenth centuries, we come across many characters who did not believe their work was ordained by God and had something of a romantic temperament, which Eric Stokes defined as a combination of a strong introspective bent, a sensibility for natural beauty and for historical associations, with an imaginative urge for release in action and adventure. Much of their interest lay in their respect for India, for its people and their way of life. A brief sketch of some of these colourful sahibs is given below:

JOB CHARNOCK

The East India Company's agent in Bengal in the seventeenth century, Job Charnock is better known as the founder of Calcutta, the city which was to become the capital of the Indian Empire and one of the largest cities in the world. Without any notable family background or education Charnock was a man of stubborn determination and vision. He came to Bengal in 1655 and worked his way up to become the chief of the Company's factory in 1663. He had the audacity to declare war on the Mughal Empire in 1686 over a quarrel about customs dues. Though outnumbered in force he employed clever tactics to compel the Mughal army to seek a truce. It was after this triumph that he chose the site of Calcutta at the behest of his Hindu wife Rani, for the sake of a large shady tree. A momentous event of his life was his marriage to a young Hindu girl of fifteen whom he rescued from the funeral pyre of her husband when she was about to commit sati. Her extraordinary beauty, arrayed in her finest drapery and decked with ornaments to symbolize the end of her worldly existence, struck Charnock. It is not known whether he married her under either Christian or Hindu rites, but presumably he formed a lifelong romantic alliance with her, as was the common practice in those times. She bore Charnock three daughters—Mary, Elizabeth and Catherine. As such unions were permanent the children were often treated as members of the family. At that period, Indian wives were given due respect and affection by the English society in India. Some high-ranking Company officers with Indian wives used to send their children for education to England where they were often assimilated. Charnock's eldest daughter Mary married Sir Eyre Coote, one of the Company's celebrated generals who later became commander-in-chief. Three British prime ministers, the two Pitts and Lord Liverpool, according to an Anglo-Indian historian Frank Anthony, had some Indian blood.

Charnock's wife died soon after the foundation of Calcutta and he was overwhelmed with grief. His attachment to her was so great that according to a contemporary account he would sacrifice a fowl on her death anniversary at her mausoleum. This practice was apparently derived from some local Hindu rites in Bihar from where she was rescued. Charnock also died in 1693, having reigned more absolutely than a raja. He was recognized as one of the most formidable of the early English administrators. Both Charnock and his wife lie buried in the churchyard of St. Johns Church, Calcutta, commemorated by an impressive mausoleum.

George Thomas—Jehaz Sahib

A fluent linguist in Persian and Hindi both written and spoken, George Thomas was a colourful character who won fame and fortune as a swashbuckling mercenary. He led an extraordinary adventurous life until his death in 1802 and lies buried in Berhampur in the same cemetery as the first wife of Warren Hastings. Born in Ireland in 1756, he became a sailor but deserted his ship at Madras and turned into a soldier of fortune. He impressed the south Indian ruling princes as a trainer of cavalry. Still in his twenties, he then discovered bright prospects as a mercenary with the Marathas and moved to north India where they were extending their power and influence. It was however his encounter with Begum Sumroo that brought him into prominence. He managed to rescue the Begum from captivity when she was held in chains at Sardana by her mutinous troops. With his tiny body of troops facing odds of over four to one, it was a very brave venture indeed. Thomas the adventurer-cum-paramour was generously rewarded by the Begum and also provided with one of her harem beauties as a wife.

Thomas continued his pursuits, amassing wealth through extortion by way of protection money from the weak rajas in the neighbouring territories. At the zenith of his career in 1797, he came to be known as King Thomas, a white raja who proclaimed himself dictator of all the territories south of the Sutlej belonging to the Sikhs. A mercenary to the core, he enjoyed fighting but maintained his loyalty both to the Begum and the British Crown. The East India Company was always keen to hire the services of such military adventurers who maintained their own trained cavalry troops.

Thomas was given an Indian nickname of Jehaz Sahib, derived perhaps from his name George, or from the Hindustani word jehaz, ship, referring to his being a sailor when he landed in Madras. Around 1800, he decided to return home to enjoy a nabob's life there. Unfortunately, he did not reach Calcutta to catch the ship as he died on the way. On learning about his death, his loyal troops were so heartbroken that they declined to serve any other officer and decided to renounce the worldly life and turn into mendicants.

COLONEL JOHN COLLINS

From the middle of the eighteenth century, as the British acquired political power and prestige, they installed their residents in the courts of Indian princes. Some British residents adopted opulent lifestyles, a queer mixture of Eastern glitter and European supremacy. In the early nineteenth century, Colonel John Collins, at the court of the Maratha prince the Scindia Maharaja, was one such character. Nicknamed King Collins, he lacked both diplomacy and statecraft but assumed an overbearing manner. In tune with the contemporary practice he behaved like a Mughal nawab and kept a well-staffed zenana. He travelled accompanied by his zenana and an escort, which included a brigade of artillery to fire salute to him and also a large suite of tents and other paraphernalia, which might have served for the great Mughal. Though his entourage was impressive, Collins was described as

> . . . an insignificant little odd-looking man dressed in an old-fashioned military coat, white breeches, sky-blue silk stockings and with large glaring buckles on his shoes, and having his highly powdered wig from which descended a pigtail of no ordinary dimensions surmounted by a small round black silk hat ornamented with a single black ostrich feather looking altogether not unlike a monkey dressed up for Bartholomew.

However, despite his odd appearance, Collins made up with an aggressive manner with which he handled the Company's affairs but failed to influence the Scindia who refused to sign a treaty presented by Collins on behalf of the Company. In 1806, he was moved to the residency at Lucknow where he died one year later.

GENERAL SIR DAVID OCHTERLONY—LOONY AKHTAR

One of the most outstanding soldier–administrator–diplomats, General Ochterlony's achievements won him the admiration of both his countrymen and Indians. A powerful personality, he looked upon India with due respect and believed in administering on a principle of humility not pride. He believed that Indian princely states should be preserved as places where Indian culture could flourish in its natural milieu. It was for both his popularity and achievements that a 165-foot monument, which still stands, was erected in his honour in the centre of Calcutta. The inscription at the base of this extraordinary structure—in style part Syrian, part Turkish, part Egyptian—states: 'The people of India, native and European, to commemorate his services as a statesman, and a soldier, have in grateful admiration raised this column.'

Born in Boston 1758, Ochterlony came to India in 1778 to join the East India Company as a soldier. By dint of hard work and intelligence, he rose in the Company's hierarchy and was twice British resident of Delhi. He lived in and around Delhi from the time of

Sir David Ochterlony

its capture in 1803 till his death at Meerut in 1825. Also addressed as Loony Akhtar he lived in royal Indian style, with Mughal pomp, maintaining a herd of thirteen elephants to carry an equal number of his Indian wives. He entertained both Indians and Europeans lavishly with nautch performances by the most accomplished nautch girls of Delhi. He built several mansions in Delhi and other places. Accompanied by a retinue of both European and Indian servants and an escort of smartly uniformed cavalry, with his baggage transported on several elephants and camels, he travelled like an oriental prince. The private tents of his zenana were set up in a large enclosure with red cloth hung around to inhibit the gaze of people. He was a generous patron of local artists, and became a legendary figure of Delhi. A well-known painting by a Delhi artist portrays him in Indian dress, smoking a hookah and watching a nautch in his house at Delhi.

GENERAL WILLIAM PALMER

Perhaps the most well-known case of an Englishman having two Indian wives, both of Mughal descent, was that of General William Palmer. He joined the East India Company in 1766 and rose to become the ADC and military secretary to Governor General Warren Hastings. It was probably in 1781 that Palmer married under Muslim law Bibi Faiz Baksh, a princess of the Delhi royal house. It was common practice for the sahibs at that time to have Indian wives or bibis and raise families who were accepted by English society. Bibi Faiz Baksh was bestowed the title of Begum by the Mughal emperor Shah Alam; the sanat granting her this title is preserved in the British Library in London. She bore Palmer six children—four boys and two girls. Palmer was deeply attached to her and lived with her until his death in 1816. In his will, he referred to her as Bibi Faiz Baksh Sahiba who has been my affectionate friend and companion during a period of more than thirty-five years. It is recorded that Palmer married a second wife, a princess of the Avadh house. Another story says that he married the sister of Faiz Baksh. His second wife is said to have died in Hyderabad in 1828 and was buried in the Palmer's cemetery there. The famous painting of the Palmer family by British artist Francesco Renaldi is held by the British Library. Later, Palmer was appointed resident at the Maratha Peshwa's court in Poona and in 1801 he was made a general in charge of the Monghyr command. His family established the famous banking house of the Palmers. They built up such a successful banking business that they could lend up to one million pounds to the Nizam when he needed it. His granddaughter married Colonel Meadows Taylor, the famous author of the *Confessions of a Thug*.

It is interesting to note that in the 1920s Palmer's great-granddaughter was critical of him for having had two wives.

Colonel James Skinner—Sikander Sahib

The celebrated military adventurer and founder of the famous Skinners Horse Cavalry Regiment, James Skinner was in his time the most colourful personality of Delhi. Born in 1778, he was the son of a Scotsman, Hercules Skinner, who rose to the rank of lieutenant colonel. His mother was the daughter of a Rajput landlord. He

James Skinnner, founder of the famous Skinner Horse regiment of the British Indian Army (by a Delhi artist from the Skinners' album, c. 1820)

became a victim of the East India Company's policy which debarred Anglo-Indians from military service with Company troops. In 1795, at the age of seventeen, he joined the Maratha army. In recognition of his valour and for saving the Maratha ruler Scindia's life, the maharaja generously rewarded him. Later, he was persuaded to accept command of irregular cavalry serving with the Company's forces. The British were greatly impressed by his commanding skill and popularity with his troops. Indians knew him as Sikander Sahib, Hindustani for Alexander the Great. Skinner raised his own cavalry regiment, Skinner's Horse or 'The Yellow Boys' since they wore yellow uniforms. In due course, Skinner's Horse became part of the Indian army and its most prestigious regiment of the armoured corps. In 1826, on the recommendation of the government, Skinner was made Commander of the Bath and also given the rank of lieutenant colonel. He was one of the few Anglo-Indians to make a name for himself and command the respect of both the British and the Indians. He had an estate at Hansi and a large house at Kashmiri Gate in Delhi which was a place of lavish entertainment for both Indians and Europeans. All high-ranking Company officials and other travelling dignitaries, including the Governor General, have left fascinating accounts about Skinner's extraordinary hospitality. Hailed as one of the bravest and most distinguished soldiers in the Company's army, he was also praised for his charities for public institutions and needy people. A perfect gentleman, he was admired for his integrity and generosity. He lived in semi-Indian style and maintained a zenana of seven wives and is said to have sired eighty children. He built the famous St James Church in Delhi and also a mosque and a temple for his wives. He has been described as short, sturdily built and dark in complexion. Apart from being a great soldier and leader of men, Skinner was a

Persian scholar and wrote his memoirs in that language. He was also a great patron of artists. His nautch parties were most popular and he took delight in presenting to his guests pictures of the dancing girls entertaining them with their performance. He commissioned several Indian artists to work for him and his two famous albums are held by the British Library—one carrying illustrations of his friends from the nobility and princely families and the second of the common people with their castes and occupations.

WILLIAM FRASER

Born in 1784, William Fraser came to India to work for the East India Company. He distinguished himself at the Fort William College at Calcutta and joined as secretary to the resident at Delhi in 1805. After taking part in the Nepal war of 1814–15 he returned to Delhi for the rest of his career, administering the north-western provinces. He took over in 1833 as civil commissioner and agent to the Governor General, the new designation for the post of resident. He became a vegetarian and had quickly acquired Indian ways. He was an intelligent linguist and mixed more with Indians than with his British colleagues. He lived happily in Delhi in the company of his seven native wives and enjoyed throwing lavish nautch parties. In 1812, Lady Nugent, wife of the commander-in-chief in Calcutta, was shocked and surprised at Fraser's lifestyle and even reprimanded him for neglecting his religion. The famous French botanist Victor Jaquemont described him as 'half Asiatic in his habits but in other respects a Scotch highlander and an excellent man with great originality of thought, a metaphysician to boot and enjoying the best possible reputation of being a country

bear'. Fraser was a generous patron of Delhi artists
as revealed by the family papers discovered in 1979.
This vast collection includes pictures of costumes and
occupations as well as true-to-life portraits of Fraser's
Indian friends, local villagers and his office staff. These
paintings are now recognized as the finest examples of
Company paintings. Outstanding for their realism and
sensitivity, some of these portraits carry inscriptions
by Fraser, identifying the persons. The pictures also
throw light on Fraser's private life. There is one of a
beautiful Indian woman with a child inscribed in Persian,
'Sarwan—a Jaat woman, the chosen one of Fraser Sahib
whose delicate beauty was beyond compare'. Like other
famous sahibs, Fraser enjoyed Indian luxuries with his
bibis and children. He supplemented his income with
earnings from a horse-breeding farm in partnership with
his close friend Colonel James Skinner. Fond of nautch
parties he commissioned the artist Lalji and his son
Hulaslal to come to his house and make portraits of
his favourite nautch girls, Malagire, Kandarbaksh and
Pyarijan. The Aga Khan Gallery in Geneva is now in
possession of these paintings. In spite of his popularity,
one of his judgements in a land dispute enraged the
aggrieved party and he was assassinated on the streets
of Delhi in 1835. The assassin, son of William's horse-
dealing partner, the nawab of Ferozepur, was caught
and hanged.

GENERAL CLAUDE MARTIN

A French military adventurer Claude Martin joined the
British army after the fall of Pondicherry in 1761 and
became a military commander of the Avadh nawab.
Towards the late eighteenth century, Lucknow had

emerged as a flourishing cultural centre, attracting many international adventurers to settle in Lucknow with the patronage of Nawab Shuja-ud-daula who was greatly influenced by the Western way of life, even their clothes. Martin made a fortune from the indigo business and other profitable ventures, including sale of European novelties at exorbitant prices to the nawab. He lived in great style and maintained four bibis, several eunuchs and a host of slaves. Fond of art and literature, he had a vast collection of books and manuscripts in Latin, French, English, Persian and Sanskrit. He was also a great patron of artists and in his gallery were hung one hundred and fifty oil paintings, including works by famous British artists Zoffany and Daniel. A French bon vivant who combined business acumen with ideas of grandeur, Martin built a magnificent palace in Lucknow. According to a contemporary account, his house was

> built on the bank of the river Gomti and boats passed under the room in which he dined. He has underground apartments, even with the edge of the water, the most comfortable in the world in the hot weather and the most elegantly decorated. As the water rises he ascends; the lower storey is always flooded in the rains and the second generally; when the water subsides they are repaired and redecorated . . . it would require a week at least to examine the contents of his house.

He and other European adventurers in Lucknow lived in ostentatious style far exceeding the luxuriousness of their days in Calcutta; they dined alternately with each other and kept a band to play who had learned English and Scotch airs.

Martin was also generous in looking after the upbringing of children with Indian mothers left behind

by the sahibs on their return to Europe. Of all these
children his special favourite was one young girl Bulone
or Lise who came under his care in 1775 at the age
of nine. Martin is said to have purchased her from a
Frenchman who in turn had given her asylum when
she fled her home following the killing of her sister
by her father Nawab Fazl Khan. Martin offered to
arrange a suitable marriage for her as she grew up but
by then Bulone got so attached to him that she chose
to become his bibi. Martin reciprocated her attachment
and arranged her learning Persian and provided her with
full facilities to enable her to pursue her religion. He
was moved by her devotion and he 'loved her as the
most chaste virtuous wife'. Bulone outlived Martin by
thirty-four years and one of her duties was the rearing
of another of his adopted children James Martin or
Zulfikar Khan. When Martin died in 1800, he left him
a pension on condition that he acted as manager for all
of Martin's female dependents. Most of his wealth was
used to establish the two La Martiniere institutions, one
in Lucknow and the other in Lyons in France.

Select Bibliography

Acland, Rev. T.A. *Popular Account of the Manners and Customs of India*, London, 1847.

Archer, M. *British Drawings in the India Office Library*, 2 vols, London, 1969.

—— *Company Drawings in the India Office Library*, London, 1972—*India and British Portraiture*: 1770–1825, London, 1979.

Bacon, Thomas. *First Impressions*, 2 vols, London, 1837.

Baden-Powell, R.S.S. *Pigsticking or Hoghunting*, London, 1889.

Ballhatchet, K. *Race, Sex, and Class under the Raj*, New York, 1980.

Bellew, Capt. *Memoirs of a Griffin*, London, 1843.

Belnos, Mrs. S.C. *Twenty-four Plates Illustrative of Hindu and European Manners in Bengal*, London, 1832.

Bernier, F. *Travels in the Mughal Empire, 1656–1668*, London, 1891.

Braddon, E. *Thirty Years of Shikar*, Edinburgh, 1895.

Broughton, T.D. *Letters Written in a Mahratta Camp during the year 1809*, London, 1892.

Brown, H., ed. *The Sahibs, The Life and Ways of the British in India as Recorded by Themselves*, London, 1948.

Busteed, H.E. *Echoes from old Calcutta*, Calcutta, 1888.

Bulter, W. *The Land of Veda*, New York, 1873.

Carey, W.H. *The Good Old Days of Honourable John Company*, Calcutta, 1964.

Caunter Rev. Hobart. *Oriental Annual*, London 1834–1839.

Cheem Aliph. *Lays of Ind*, 7th edition, Calcutta, 1883.

Craufurd, Q. *Sketches—Chiefly Relating to the History, Religion, Learning and Manners of the Hindus*, London, 1790.

Dodwell, H.H. *The Nabobs of Madras*, London, 1926.

D'Oyly, C. *Tom Raw, The Griffin*, London, 1828.

—— *The Costumes and Customs of Modern India*, London, c 1824.

—— *The European in India*, London, 1813.

Dubois, A.J.A. *Hindu Manners, Customs and Ceremonies*, Oxford, 1968 Reprint.

Dyson, K.K. *A Various Universe—A Study of the Journals and Memoirs of British Men and Women in the Indian Subcontinent*, Oxford, 1978.

Eden, Emily. *Up the Country*, ed. H. Lawrence, London, 1901

Edwards, M. *Glorious Sahibs*, London, 1968.

—— *The Sahibs and the Lotus*, London, 1988.

Edwin, A. *India Revisited*, London, 1886. British India (1772–1947), London,

Elwood, A.K. *Narrative of a Journey Overland from England by the Continent of Europe, Egypt and the Red Sea, to India*, 2 vols, London, 1830.

Forbes, J. *Oriental Memoirs*, 4 vols, London 1813.

Forster, G. *Sketches of the Mythology and Customs of the Hindoos*, London, 1785.

Foster, William ed. *Early Travels in India*. Reprinted, Delhi, 1968.

Frost, Thomas, *Lives of the Conjurores*, London, 1876.

Gay, J.D. *From Pall Mall to the Punjab*, London, 1876.

Graham, M. *Journal of a Residence in India*, Edinburgh, 1813.

Grose, J.H. A *Voyage to the East Indies*, London, 1766.

Hall, Capt. Basil. *Travels in India*, London, 1931.

Hart, W.H. *Everyday Life in Bengal and Other Indian Sketches*, London, 1906.

Heber, R. *Narrative of a Journey through the Upper Provinces of India from Calcutta to Bombay*. 2 vols, London, 1828.

Hervey, H. *The European in India*, London, 1913.

Hicks, F.C. *Forty Years among the Wild Animals of India*, Allahabad, 1910.

Hogdes, W. *Travels in India during the Years 1780–83*, London, 1793.

Hyam, R. *British Imperial Century*, London, 1976.

Johnson, Daniel. *Sketches of Indian Field Sports*, London, 1827.

Kaul, H.K. *Travellers' India, An Anthology*, New Delhi, 1979.

Kerr, S. *Selections from Calcutta Gazette*, 6 vols, Calcutta, 1864.

Kincaid, D. *British Social Life in India*, London, 1938.

Kindersley, Mrs N. *Letter from the East Indies*, London, 1977.

Kipling, J.L. *Beast and Man in India*, London, 1891.

Kisch, H.M. *A Young Victorian in India*, London, 1957.

Knighton, W. *Trophical Sketches*, 2 vols, London, 1855.

—— *The Private Life of an Eastern King*, London, 1856.

Martyn, H. *Bengal Past and Present*, London, 1837.

Moorhouse, G. *India Britannica*, London, 1983.

Mundy, G.C. *Pen and Pencil Sketches*, 2 vols, London, 1832.

Murray's (publishers) *A Handbook for Travellers in India, Burma and Ceylon, including all British India, the Portuguese and French Possessions, and the Indian States*, 13th edn., London and Calcutta 1929.

Nevile, Pran. *Love Stories from the Raj*, New Delhi, 1995.

—— *Nautch Girls of India*, New Delhi, 1996.

Nugent, Maria, *A Journal from the Year 1811 to the Year 1815*, London, 1984.

Pal, P. and Dehejia, V. *From Merchants to Emperors*, New York, 1986.

Parks, Fanny, *Wanderings of a Pilgrim in Search of the Picturesque* 2 vols, London, 1850.

Princeep, V.C. *Imperial India*, London, 1879.

Quiz. *The Grand Master or Adventures of Qui Hi*, London, 1816.

Raghuvanshi, V.P.S. *Indian Society in the 18th Century*, New Delhi, 1969.

Rousselet, L. *India and its Native Princes*, London, 1875.

Savory, Isabel, *A Sportswoman in India*, London, 1900.

Sherwood, Mrs. M.M. *The Life and Times of Mrs. Sherwood* (1775–1851) ed. by F.J. Harvey, Darton, London, 1910.

The History of George Desmond, London, 1821.

Siegel, Lee. *Net of Magic*, Chicago, 1991.

Skinner, Capt. T. *Excursions in India*, 2 vols, London.

Sleeman, W.H. *Rambles and Reflections of an Indian Official*, 2 vols, London, 1844.

—— *A Journey* through the Kingdom of Oudh, 2 vols, London, 1858.

Smith, Robert. *Pictorial Journal of Travels in Hindustan from 1828 to 1833*, Unpublished manuscript. Victoria and Albert Museum, London.

Solvyns, B. *Les Hindous*, 4 vols, Paris, 1808–1812.

Torrens, H.D. *Travels in Ladakh, Tartary and Kashmir*, London, 1862.

Williamson, T. *The East India Vade Mecum*, 2 vols. London 1810

—— *Oriental Field Sports*, 2 vols, London, 1819.

Woodruff, P. *The Men Who Ruled India*, 2 vols, London, 1963.